Transcendental Sex

TRANSCENDENTAL SEX

A Meditative Approach to Increasing Sensual Pleasure

by Jerry Gillies

Drawings by Teri L. Misrach

Holt, Rinehart and Winston   New York

Copyright © 1978 by Jerry Gillies
Drawings copyright © 1978 by Teri L. Misrach
All rights reserved, including the right to reproduce this book or portions thereof in any form.

Published simultaneously in Canada by Holt, Rinehart and Winston of Canada, Limited.

Library of Congress Cataloging in Publication Data

Gillies, Jerry, 1940–
Transcendental sex.

1. Sex (Psychology)   2. Transcendental meditation.
I. Title.
BF692.G54   301.4.'8   77-15202
ISBN 0-03-021996-5

Designer: Joy Chu

Printed in the United States of America
1 3 5 7 9 10 8 6 4 2

Grateful acknowledgment is made to Marjorie K. Toomim, Ph.D., and Hershel Toomim for permission to quote from their paper "The Experience of Love."

*To Bonnie Cousins
and
Ma Anand Rupa,
with love and
deep appreciation*

One a lover, one a friend.
May the cycle never end.

CONTENTS

Acknowledgments   ix
Preface   xi
1   *The Quiet Excitement   1*
2   *Inner Strengths   9*
3   *Flowing Freely   27*
4   *Sharing Energy   63*
5   *Transcendental Arousal   93*
6   *The Loving Connection   118*
7   *Letting Go and Afterglow   136*
8   *The Transcendental Sex Ritual   154*

ACKNOWLEDGMENTS

No book is the product of a single person, and this work has been supported, enhanced, and inspired by a number of friends and colleagues. Words alone cannot express my gratitude to the artist, Teri L. Misrach, for so beautifully transcending the challenge I put before her. A warm hug to Barbara Davis, who has been a special source of strength and ideas, and another to Vicki Johnson, who has been there during the most critical period with feedback and a warm shoulder. For their friendship, enthusiasm, and creative stimulation, deep thanks to Michael Blate, Carole Geffen, Diana Lippin, Ron and Jan Parks, and Susan Leff.

I've been especially fortunate to have learned much from five friends who are very knowledgeable in the area of human sexuality: Carole Altman, my former partner in the Biofeedback Institute of New York and author of *You Can Be Your Own Sex Therapist*; Dr. Herbert Otto and Roberta Otto, authors of *Total Sex*; and Drs. Claude and Dorothy Nolte, authors of *Wake Up In Bed Together*. Special thanks to photographer Robert D. Freedman for his efforts in preparing the illustrations, and to Dr. Mary Ann Somervill for her invaluable technical assistance. Most importantly, this book would not have been possible without the constant feedback, support, and suggestions from the many men and women who have attended my workshops and read my books and have been willing to share their responses.

PREFACE

If I were asked why I wrote this book, I would respond, half tongue-in-cheek: because no else has done it. Surprisingly, in these liberated 1970s, no other attempt has yet been made to unify meditation with sensual and sexual relating in a book designed for our Western culture. Yet in the countless workshops and seminars I've conducted, it has been exactly those changes brought about through meditation that have transformed ordinary love lives into something more intense and satisfying. Transcendental Sex brings meditation and sexuality together and, audacious as it sounds, aims at nothing less than the complete transformation of all our individual and societal attitudes about human sexuality.

Social scientists looking back on this period from a point sometime in the future will surely come to the conclusion that we Homo sapiens underwent some powerful spiritual and consciousness changes in the seventh and eighth decades of the twentieth century. Meditation, exploration of altered states of consciousness, concern for the outer environment, increasing individual knowledge about the inner workings of the human body, a move away from purely material accomplishment as the only goal in life—all have greatly increased human awareness.

Sexuality is perhaps the last vital area to be affected. Here, we cannot really claim to have evolved in proportion to our potential. This may be due to the fact that much of our past cultural and parental conditioning has built up inhibitions in this important facet of human experience and behavior. We therefore carry around a lot of negative emotional programming about sex and our own sexuality. Education, information, and the liberation of women from second-class sexual status have done much in recent years to counter this ignorance. Perhaps we are now ready to leave the minus column, start at point zero, and begin our ascent to transcendence.

Though the concept has been distorted throughout the centuries, most of the great religions of the world have viewed sexual union between a man and a woman as a sacred act, reaffirming our connection with God. In this view, sex is a gift from God, a way of experiencing and perpetuating the life force, a physical celebration of the spiritual. Sex has an inherent spirituality only waiting to be awakened in each individual. This book is designed to help you experience that quality in your sexual functioning, and to remove obstacles from your path to transcendental sexual union. In so doing, it will sensitize your entire system so as to provide a quantum leap in the amount of pleasure you experience.

The dictionary definition of *transcendental* is: surpassing or superior, being beyond ordinary or common experience, rising above, outdoing or exceeding in excellence, going past ordinary limits. Transcendental Sex is designed to provide you with tools to use your sexual and sensual potential to the fullest, to rise above the limitations that have been holding you back, to move on to new heights in sensitivity, pleasure, and intensity.

There are three major premises in this book: first, that meditation can greatly enhance your sexual life; second, that sex can become, in itself, a powerful meditation; and third, that realizing the spiritual and meditative aspects of your own sexuality can be a transcendent experience.

Sex is, of course, far from a mere physical act. It fully engages the mind as well as the body, and it affects the entire being. In recent years, the Western world has seen a dramatic increase in the popularity of meditation and various meditative techniques, including the largest organized effort, Transcendental Meditation. In fairness to the TM people, I should mention that Transcendental Sex has nothing to do with that movement, though I have had many TM graduates in my classes and workshops and have always found them quickly adaptive to my approach and techniques. With all of this interest, however, little attention has been paid to the Eastern or spiritual approach to sex. There is Tantra, of course, the yoga of sex, but even this has been paid very little attention. Many people have heard that such a thing exists, but real knowledge is limited, and the application of that knowledge is almost unheard of. The available books on Tantra, for example, spend a lot of time on very elaborate and complex mind/body disciplines, and tend only to confuse those who seek simple ways to enhance their own sexual experience through a meditative or spiritual approach. Adding to the confusion is the fact that there are many different forms of Tantra, including those in the Hindu, Buddhist, and Tibetan traditions. While Transcendental Sex does adapt some material from the Tantric, it is really quite different in many ways. Tantra, for instance, focuses a lot of attention on remaining sexually connected without movement and without orgasm. This may be interesting as an occasional experiment, but I feel as a way of life it is exploitative, using sex to reach some spiritual goal. Transcendental Sex is the absence of any predetermined goals, whether these involve the desire for an orgasm or the desire to avoid one. A healthier and more loving attitude is to enjoy what is happening, wherever it leads. Another Tantric focus is on the superiority of the male. To some extent, in many Tantric practices, the woman is only a vessel, a means for the man to achieve his spiritual growth. Transcendental Sex believes in the liberation of both sexes from rigid gender roles, not from any moral or liberal doctrine but just because it feels so much better. You can't have total union between two people unless you have two whole people. Transcendental Sex doesn't pretend to be completely new, and it borrows freely from the Eastern concepts when this seems appropriate. But this is the first time that a Western-oriented system has been designed to add spiritual qualities to your current sexual activity, while preparing you for new levels of awareness, sensual satisfaction, and interpersonal communication.

Because I'm a firm believer in the adage that experience is the best teacher, this book is action-oriented. You will find some seventy exercises contained on these pages, each with specific instructions. These are your tools. How you use them is up to you, though I'll offer some suggestions in the first chapter. What you get out of this book will come from exploring these experiences and exercises more than from my words.

The drawings, which illustrate many of these exercises, are designed to create a mood both loving and meditative, sensual and intense, and far removed from the mechanical artificiality depicted in most books purporting to teach about sex. The man and woman are obviously two people whose genuine love and respect for each other resounds in every look and in every exchange. The words, exercises, and drawings, I hope, will come together to inspire you.

Transcendental Sex

1
THE QUIET EXCITEMENT

With a buzz and a beep and a whir, a strange spaceship descends to Earth. Two bizarre creatures emerge and float to the ground. They are a young Martian couple, both scientists, here on an exploratory visit. They decide that the best way to find out about Earth is to communicate with some of the inhabitants, so off they bounce in search of some likely candidates. They enter an apartment building in the mysterious way Martians have of doing these things, and settle upon a newly wedded couple by the names of Everett and Gladys Sprinkle (honest!). Well, Everett and Gladys are as surprised as could be, but quickly adjust, in that special way newlyweds have of adapting to startling surprises. With one thing and another, the talk finally ends up on the subject of reproduction. The Martian male astounds the Sprinkles by offering to demonstrate the way people reproduce on his planet. Before they can protest in their embarrassment, he grabs the Martian woman, places the eight chubby fingers of his single hand on her forehead, and while he sparkles and she twinkles, an opening appears in her side and a tiny baby Martian hops out and starts prancing around Everett and Gladys's living room. The Martian male then asks them how it is done on Earth. They hem and haw a bit, and finally decide that it would be too difficult to describe; so, in the interest of interplanetary cooperation, they take off their clothes and give a demonstration. The Martians watch their performance, enthralled. When it is all over, the Martian woman asks, "When will the Earthchild come out?" Gladys shakes her head and tells her that it will take nine months. The Martians are amazed at this, scratch their heads a bit, and then the male asks, "But if it isn't coming out right now, how come you were both so excited toward the end?"

The Martian had a good question. Often, the degree of frenzy exhibited is considered the true measurement of passion and satisfaction. When you think about it, however, common sense alone would dictate that you could experience more of whatever is happening physically by slowing down and paying attention. On the one hand we declare the sexual act to be one of life's greatest pleasures, while on the other we always seem to be rushing to get it over with. In our culture, we seem to spend much of our energy rushing toward the orgasm, which, after all, is the end of the sexual experience for most people. Perhaps we are so conditioned to feel guilt and inhibition over the sex act that, at some subconscious level, we are determined to have it done and over as quickly as possible.

Those in the Eastern cultures have known for thousands of years the value of "quiet excitement"—the slowing down of sexual functioning to enhance perception and heighten pleasure. Transcendental Sex is an effort to take some of these ancient traditions and use them as guidelines to develop a new way of looking at the sexual experience. Not to reach satori or oneness with God, not to use one's sexual partner to attain a self-centered spiritual "high," but to give greater pleasure to each other, reach new dimensions in sensual communication, and intensely appreciate what harmony and flowing can do to enrich physical satisfaction. This is not to say that you won't experience a religious or spiritual quality to your sexual union; but this has to be allowed to happen, and cannot be a preselected aspiration. The primary purpose of Transcendental Sex is to allow fuller enjoyment of the sensual and sexual potential we all have, and to realize that the more we experience our unlimited capacity in this area, the more human and sensitive and loving we become.

Loving and Trusting Your Body

Certain responses are built into your physiological system. They don't need to be pushed; they don't need to be rushed. Your body knows how to gratify itself, it knows what it needs to feel complete and satisfied. If you would just stop trying to control it with your mind, just relax and enjoy it, just trust it, you would be well on the road to a transcendental love life. This also means loving your body and appreciating its magnificence. Your body is a gigantic instrument of love. The offering of a body you love is a much greater gift to your partner than that of a body you neglect, don't appreciate, and have let become undernourished in terms of loving attention. Loving and trusting your body will allow you to see more clearly the advantages of the quiet excitement of Transcendental Sex, for this will be a way for you to spend more time nurturing yourself, giving and receiving caressing strokes. Your skin is your largest organ, and it has a voracious appetite for touch sensations; it is starved into frustration by the touch-deprived lives most people live.

Thoughtlessness

In Transcendental Sex terms, thoughtlessness means the absence of conscious thought, and it is a highly desirable aspiration. Meditation is thoughtlessness, shutting off the thinking process, so that you may delve deeper into your own consciousness. When you return to thinking from a meditative state, that thinking is usually clearer, and more creative, as if you had given your brain a refreshing bath to clear the cobwebs and debris away. In sex, for instance, you develop practical skills not by focusing your thoughts on what comes next or remembering some fancy technique, but by letting thoughts go and allowing your senses to absorb whatever comes in. If your body does not like what is happening, it will automatically change and try something else. It's again a question of trusting your body, and realizing that your computerlike brain is a storehouse of images that bring you all your practical knowledge. These images can be useful only when they are received clearly. A head filled with thoughts interferes with that clear reception. Fear and doubt can also get in the way. This learning process is the same for any activity. The best way to improve your skills in all actions involving the body is to learn to let go of the mind, to enter into unthinking spontaneity. And this is meditation. Rather than being anti-intellectual, it sharpens your intellectual powers by giving your mind a needed rest once in a while, by giving you the skill to turn your thoughts on or off—a powerful mind accomplishment.

The Power of Sex

In many ancient spiritual traditions, sexual union was considered the highest state man and woman could attain, the closest to the divine bliss that anyone could hope to achieve; in uniting the male and female energies of life, some cosmic force was released. In a sense, we have all experienced this cosmic force, moments of sheer ecstasy that elevated us and expanded our consciousness. These are usually fleeting moments, and sometimes frightening, since they give us a brief glimpse into the unknown, a taste of something beyond physical reality. Transcendental Sex can help unveil the mystery by giving you an understanding of this basic life force as natural and organic. Scientists are even now researching the indefinable energy exchange that takes place when two people make love. But it isn't necessary to understand its exact nature to enjoy it. As you quiet down your mind and body, and reach a calm emotional state, this power will emerge and carry you into new sensations and heightened states of consciousness. Relish it, allow it to wash over you as a warm tide; but don't try to analyze it, for this will only lead to frustration and interrupted experience.

Grace and Beauty

Another focus of Transcendental Sex is aesthetic in nature. The lovemaking of many people resembles nothing so much as a wrestling match. Often small children who happen to see their father and mother in the sex act think something violent is happening. It looks violent, it looks like a fight. It is ugly, not beautiful. The act of love deserves better than this. The two partners should be dancing together, not fighting. Their movements can be harmonious, with the grace of a slow-motion scene. Look at the drawings in this book. The man and woman are in harmony, seeking to share fully with each other. It should be noted here that the purpose of Transcendental Sex isn't to switch from rapid sexual movements or intense pelvic thrusts to mild and slow actions. That would merely be substituting one rigid pattern in sexual functioning for another. This approach is primarily designed to enhance pleasure, to provide new alternatives in sexual relating, to increase the possibilities of peak fulfillment. There is nothing "wrong" with rapid and spasmodic thrusts during intercourse, but it isn't the only way to build sexual energy, and it may even be the least effective way of all. Just as we have learned from the Eastern martial arts that wildly attacking an opponent with a lot of misused and misdirected energy is not nearly as effective as the smooth, fluid movements of someone trained in a meditative system of quieting the mind and the body, we can learn that sexual success and satisfaction for both partners comes not from how fast and tense we are, but from how aware and sensitive we are. It isn't to create a sophisticated image that a wine connoisseur very slowly savors the initial taste and smell of the liquid, and then quietly sips it until the final drop; it is rather to produce much greater pleasure and much keener taste sensations.

Your Partner

Transcendental Sex is a most intimate sharing experience. Ideally, your partner should be someone for whom you have deep feelings of love, someone with whom you feel free to expose your vulnerability, free to let yourself go. You are about to engage in a passionate blending of energy, an intense merging of male and female forces. So your partner should be someone you wish to become a part of you, someone you will allow to absorb a part of you. Transcendental Sex is for lovers, not casual sexual partners. You don't have to be married, or even in an exclusive relationship; but, for it to really happen, you must share genuine care for each other. And your partner must be as willing as you to explore these experiences. Transcendental Sex is not something you should try to talk someone into. If your potential partner cannot see the desirability of embarking on this adventure after browsing through this book, then you are wasting your time. Sensitivity is as much a part of the choosing of a partner as it is a part of the actual process of sensual interaction. Someone who thinks a meditative approach to sex is useless or silly will obviously not be able to let go completely in these experiences. At the very least, you should both have an attitude of looking forward to something new that you will be doing together. It may be worthwhile noting here that, in Eastern sexual meditation, sometimes months and years of individual preparation are required before the student is considered ready to practice with a partner. Transcendental Sex has greatly reduced that time factor with new techniques, and has been designed to be more in tune with the quickly adaptive Western mind; but it still requires some time. That is why we start out with individual awareness and meditation exercises in the next chapter, and why I suggest you select your partner carefully.

Transcendental Sex in Action

The heart of this approach is in the many exercises and sharing experiences you are invited to explore. Both risk and responsibility are involved here. You take a risk each time you try something new; the more willing you are to take that risk, and the less attached you are to a specific result, the better it will all turn out.

Select your own setting for the experiences. You may want to be in the bedroom, or the living room, or even outdoors if privacy is possible. Your time together should be undisturbed. You may want to add to the environment with music, incense, flowers, candlelight—whatever appeals to you. If you cannot get into the mood, simply acknowledge that fact and save it for another time. If you haven't had sexual release for several weeks, meditative-sensual relating will be difficult and inappropriate. Don't be anxious if you feel yourself getting aroused during a touching or meditative exercise. Enjoy what the moment brings you, for you cannot change what is, you can only respond to it. If an orgasm happens, let it, it is what your body needed at that moment; you can always get back to the touching and sharing and meditating. With Transcendental Sex, you are encouraged to be free, and sexy, and loving, and touchable. Restrictions are unhealthy for your mind and your body, so leave them behind.

On the subject of orgasm, the Transcendental Sex view is that, unless there is a premature ejaculation problem, it should not be intentionally delayed in order to prolong pleasure. Such a delay carries with it the negative assumption that pleasure has to end with orgasm. A number of the exercises suggest that it is all right to be aroused and let that arousal subside. This is true, for it provides a new experience in sensual awareness. But when an orgasm wants to happen, let go. Thinking of the stock market report in order to take your mind off sex and enhance your endurance is ridiculous. It's like trying to prolong the flavor of a delicious food by adding 90 percent tasteless filler. It may seem like an economical idea, but in reality it is a poor bargain. Taking your mind off what is happening is taking your consciousness away from what is pleasing you, and it is prolonging nothing, only interrupting and delaying it. And by paying close attention, there's a good chance that your pleasure will naturally be prolonged. A meditative attitude will expand the amount of time between initial arousal and orgasm.

If an experience doesn't work for you, don't worry about it. It would be very surprising if all the upcoming exercises fit your specific sensual/sexual/meditative needs. Consider this a selection of tools, and you may pick and choose those that seem right for the occasion.

Over and over again, I will ask you to let go. Superb sex is simply simultaneous surrender. Surrender of your demands, of your rigid role, of your ego. Surrender of memory and anticipation. And with all of this surrendering, you will come to know that you really aren't giving up anything at all, but are gaining a powerful new appreciation of the you that really is.

2
INNER STRENGTHS

This whole book is about meditation. This specific chapter is about the beginning of meditation. It will help you understand this process and provide you with some practical tools so you can start using meditation to enhance your living and loving. There is nothing mystical or magical about meditation. It is the basic art of learning to use your body and your mind more efficiently. It is the process of letting go of conscious, controlled thought, letting go of self-limiting boundaries, letting go of rigid expectations, and letting go of any doubts you may have about your own competence, capacity, and ability to love. And, not surprisingly, since this is our theme, all of these very same factors are just as much a part of fulfilling sensual/sexual interaction as they are of meditation.

Meditation is the development of your focusing skills, your ability to pay attention to specific aspects of your experience. People who have sexual difficulty almost always have difficulty paying attention. Sex researchers and therapists have found, for instance, that when people have a problem achieving orgasm, there is always one of two factors present, sometimes both: muscular tension and rigidity, and the inability to shut off conscious thought. This is why an increasing number of sex therapists are recommending meditation to their clients. Meditation relaxes the muscles and teaches you to turn off conscious thought, to find the off/on switch for your thought processes. It produces a general quieting of the mind that can be applied to any number of specific activities; in Transcendental Sex, it is applied to your lovemaking. Meditation is not just sitting or lying quietly and focusing inward; that's just the first stage. It is the *application* of these focusing skills that is the actual meditation. This chapter is designed to introduce you to some basic concepts about meditation, and to begin to build your meditative skills.

The Meditative Trip

There was once a man who was searching for fulfillment in his life. He desperately wanted inner peace. He had heard about a great spiritual master who remained in isolation on an otherwise uninhabited island in the South Pacific. He became determined to seek out this great master and sit at his feet and learn how to achieve inner peace. It took two years for him to save the money and discharge all his responsibilities so that he was free to begin his quest. He flew to Hawaii, and from there chartered a boat to take him to this lonely island.

The boat ran into rough weather, and it was all he could do to keep from falling overboard. Instead of a few days, it took three weeks to reach the island. Taking a small rowboat, the man approached the island. It was fairly large and densely wooded. There were no signs of human existence anywhere to be seen. The man pushed and hacked his way through the tropical jungle. It took him three exhausting days, but he finally reached the foot of a small mountain —small but very steep. Hand over hand, he began to climb up the mountain, fiercely determined to make his way to the top, absolutely convinced that the master he was searching for had to be there. It took him two more days to reach the top of the mountain. He had kept alive by eating fruits and drinking their juices, but he had still managed to lose about twenty pounds in his five days on the island. At the top of the mountain was a small plateau, and a small straw hut. Slowly, the man crawled over to the hut and looked inside. There was no sign of recent habitation. This was too much, and, sobbing loudly, the man yelled out, "I give up!" He then collapsed at the entrance to the hut, thoroughly spent. Some time later, he heard a voice whispering in his ear, "Don't think. Just tell me what you are feeling right now." The man answered, "I feel at peace. Relaxed. I've never felt better." He opened his eyes to find himself staring into an ancient face of deep compassion and wisdom. This indeed was the master he had been seeking. He smiled, and the old man smiled and said, "Have you received the message you were seeking?" The man answered, "Yes."

Meditation is really about giving up attachment. Attachment to a goal, and attachment to thinking you know what is going to bring you fulfillment. Part of the excitement of being alive is the unfolding of the mystery of it all, the fact that we *don't* know all the answers, and never will, except perhaps at the moment of death. The point of the preceding story, and the point of this chapter, is that you have whatever answers you need right now, inside you. They may be hidden, but they are certainly there. And adopting a meditative way of life is one way to bring them out.

But meditation is more than just giving up control, giving up looking for external answers. It is, at its best, a way of life. It is not sitting still for twenty hours and contemplating your navel. It is not just doing the exercises at the end of this chapter. These things may help develop your meditative skills, but unless you use them in your everyday living and loving, they are wasted. With an appreciation of your already existent meditative powers, you can transcend anxiety, frustration, and negative thoughts and feelings. You will tune into the universe, gaining a sense of the oneness of all of us, while still understanding yourself as a unique individual. Bringing these qualities to your sensual/sexual activities will transform *them* into a meditation.

Meditation as a Sensual/Sexual Tool

Meditation helps you clear your mind and your body, absolute prerequisites for successful sexual interaction. This clearing process is really just the preliminary step, for if it is truly experienced, all that follows is actually a deep meditation, whether it be sexual intercourse or washing your dishes. By preparing yourself to pay attention, you allow yourself to feel all sensations and positive emotional responses more intensely. This cannot help but affect your entire life. And there's no question at all that the most exciting, flowing, beautiful sexual relating occurs between two whole people who are really able to pay attention to what is happening at all levels of awareness.

Meditation is not difficult. You have often meditated, even if you have never had meditative training. Meditation is not relaxation or concentration, though both are preludes to the true meditative state. You are more able to relax during meditation, and you are more able to sharply concentrate, if you so choose. But these are mere side effects, and to consider them the be-all and end-all of meditation is to limit the potential benefits.

If you imagine your mind as a river, usually quite turbulent, filled with many busy plans, thoughts, memories, you can view meditation as a gentle clearing of that river, allowing everything that fills it to flow out and softly damming one end so that nothing new floats in for a while. Many people subjectively describe their meditative experiences as a floating sensation of emptiness. You are already meditating, whether you use a specific technique—TM, for example, or hatha-yoga, or Zen, or Dr. Herbert Benson's Relaxation Response—or just let your mind go from time to time, tuning into your inner depths. Perhaps you have meditated watching a sunset, or found yourself drifting off to some new level of consciousness immediately following a powerful orgasm. In any event, you already have a certain capacity in this area, whether or not you follow any particular meditative discipline. The benefit from this powerful tool isn't, however, just in having it. Like any tool just left sitting there, it will become rusty. Transcendental Sex is an attempt to apply that tool toward enhancing your sexual pleasure and creating a special bond between you and a partner.

Meditation is more than an exercising of your brain. A number of specific physiological changes take place during meditation. As Founding Director of the Biofeedback Institute in New York, I was involved in some of the basic research in this field. I kept in close communication with a number of scientists as editor/publisher of the first internationally distributed newsletter on biofeedback from 1970 to 1972. The physiological responses that occur during meditation have been measured and proven time and again in carefully conducted studies. We know, however, that there are probably even more changes that take place, changes that have not yet been discovered or measured. Meditation, when properly experienced, reduces muscle tension. Oxygen consumption and respiratory rates decrease substantially. Heart rate slows down by an average decrease of about three beats per minute. Skin resistance increases, indicating a diminishing of anxiety and tension. Blood lactate (a substance directly related to stress, which in excessive amounts can produce anxiety attacks) decreases significantly. Perhaps the most publicized physiological changes during meditation are those that occur in brain-wave patterns. During meditation, a high degree of Alpha brain waves is produced. These occur at a frequency of eight to thirteen cycles per second, as measured by an electroencephalograph, or EEG. Increased Alpha brain waves indicate a slowing down or quieting down of the mind, which normally operates with brain waves fourteen cycles per second and above, known as Beta. Below the Alpha state lies Theta, at four to seven cycles per second. These brain waves are related to high creativity and visual images popping into the consciousness. Theta is also often produced during deep meditation. In the quieting-down process, you must pass through Alpha brain waves in order to reach Theta. If you go too far—below four cycles per second—you will fall asleep at Delta, the brain waves associated with sleep states.

What matters most, though, is how you feel when you meditate. If it's an enjoyable experience you are likely to continue it. If it becomes a chore or duty, or boring and monotonous, you are likely to give it up. Ironically enough, while teaching people to produce Alpha brain waves at the Biofeedback Institute, I noticed that these meditative frequencies most often occurred when the subject decided he or she wasn't getting anywhere and gave up. Just as in the story about the man seeking inner peace from the spiritual master, the act of letting go of a goal produced the deepest and most powerful results.

Meditation is the easiest thing you will ever do. You can fail only by trying too hard or making it too complicated. You'll get better with practice. When you decide which technique or set of methods suits you best, just keep doing it on a regular basis, and you will build your proficiency. Allowing your sexual interaction to become a meditation will greatly enhance your meditative skills, thus perpetuating this powerful personal resource.

Meditation for Enhanced Sensual Experience

The beginning of true meditation is letting go of sensory impressions. Not seeing. Not hearing. Not smelling. Not tasting. Not feeling with your skin. By doing this you go to a deeper level of consciousness, beyond physical sensation.

You could call this initial period a tuning-up time. For when you emerge, your senses are sharper than ever. Sensuality is merely heightened awareness of your sensory experiences. Meditation, in any form, enhances this awareness. This is the reason your senses seem so much sharper and clearer after any activity that is meditative in nature, whether walking on the beach, sailing on the ocean, stroking a kitten, or enjoying a loving sexual connection. This sensual enhancement will begin to happen for you as you combine the meditative exercises in this chapter with the sensual exercises in the following chapters. Don't try to do all these exercises at once. They are meant to be sampled and savored. As with all the exercises in this action-oriented book, you are invited to pick and choose those that suit you best, those that produce the most satisfying subjective results. Most of all, realize that trying hard is the antithesis of meditation and Transcendental Sex. Let it happen. Enjoy the happening!

The Primary Relaxation Experience

Over the years, I have led thousands of people through the following relaxation induction. In countless workshops and in training sessions at the Biofeedback Institute, it has proved to be the most effective and easily learned method of body/mind relaxation. You may choose to tape-record the instructions, or have a partner read them to you. This experience really combines two techniques, and they may be used separately as well as together for relaxing under any circumstances.

Part I: *Lie down on your back with arms at your sides and eyes closed. Allow your body to settle down into the most comfortable position possible.*

Check your breathing without forcing it, and be aware of how your body feels right now. Silently finish for yourself the sentence, "Right now, my body feels ———."

You're going to progressively tighten and then relax most of the muscles in your body.

Start with your feet and toes. Tighten them up as much as possible.

Then, make them tighter still. And tighter again. Now let go, let all that tension flow out of your feet as if a gentle tide of relaxation were washing over them.

Next, your lower legs and calves.

Tight. Tighter. Tighter. And let go.

Your upper legs and thighs. Tight. Tighter. Tighter. And let go.

Your genitals. Tight. Tighter. Tighter. And let all the tension go.

Your buttocks. Tight. Tighter. Tighter. And let go.

Your abdomen. Tight. Tighter. Tighter. Let go and relax.

Your chest. Tight. Tighter. Tighter. Let go.

Your shoulders. Tight. Tighter. Tighter. Let go and relax.

Your upper arms. Tight. Tighter. Tighter. And let go.

Your lower arms. Tight. Tighter. Tighter. And let all the tension go.

Your hands and fingers. Tight. Tighter. Tighter. And let it all go.

Your entire arms, from fingertips to shoulders. Tight. Tighter. Tighter. Let go.

Your neck. Tight. Tighter. Tighter. Let go and release all that tension.

Your face. Scrunch it up tight. Tighter. Tighter. Let it go.

Your entire body from head to toe. Tight. Tighter. Tighter. And let it all go.

Take a deep breath and let it out. Stretch any part of your body that wants to stretch. Silently finish for yourself the sentence, "Right now, my body feels ———."

Part II: *You are going to make a series of suggestions to yourself. Do not be concerned with whether or not you feel any of the physiological changes suggested. Just relax and go through the statements, silently asking yourself to experience each sensation, without having an investment in whether or not it actually happens. Pause briefly after each suggestion.*

My right arm is heavy.
My left arm is heavy.
My right leg is heavy.
My left leg is heavy.

My right arm is warm.
My left arm is warm.

My right leg is warm.
My left leg is warm.

My right arm is heavy and warm.
My left arm is heavy and warm.
My right leg is heavy and warm.
My left leg is heavy and warm.

My forehead is cool and calm.

My heart is calm and relaxed.
My genitals are warm and relaxed.
In the center of my body, my solar plexus is warm.
It breathes me.

Silently finish for yourself the sentence, "Right now, my body feels ⎯⎯⎯⎯."

Breathing

Your breathing is the very stuff of life. It can help you relax and focus on the present moment. It can enhance all sensual/sexual activity.

Place yourself in a comfortable position, either sitting or lying down. Place one hand on your abdomen. Breathe naturally, without forcing it. Feel your hand move in rhythm to your breathing. Allow the movement to relax you.

Sitting in a comfortable position, so that no part of your body is experiencing tension, relax for a moment. Focus on your body sensations. Exhale as completely as you can, pulling in your abdominal muscles to force all the extra air out. Refill your lungs with air very slowly, as you silently count to seven. Pause for a count of one. Then, exhale slowly and as completely as possible to a count of seven. For identification purposes, let's call this: Seven-In/Hold-One/Seven-Out. Repeat this twelve times.

Now, inhale deeply, puffing up the cheeks. Hold this breath as long as possible without feeling pain, and then pop it all out in one bursting breath through the mouth.

Next, inhale through both your nostrils to a count of seven, hold the breath for a count of two, and then exhale for a count of seven. You might choose to practice extra breath *control by slowly building up, perhaps over a few days, until you can inhale for a count of ten, hold for a count of five, exhale for a count of ten, and then keep the lungs empty for a count of five.*

Note: *There are many breathing exercises. Any book on Yoga contains dozens. These simple ones are probably the best ones to begin with. Vary them as you will.*

Opening a Channel

During this and other "image making" exercises, don't worry about how vivid the imagery is. This will come with practice, and even a fuzzy "picture" will produce positive results.

Get into as relaxed a position as possible, either sitting or lying down. Imagine that there is a bright silver channel or tube running down your body from the back of your nose to your genitals. See the channel as clearly as possible.

You're going to imagine that you can bring air down this channel, all the way to your genitals, thus clearing and opening up, making your breathing easier.

Bring air in through your nostrils, to the beginning of the channel just behind your nose. Hold it there a moment. Feel the air, its temperature; perhaps you can even imagine its color. And feel it as you let it out through your nose.

Breathe in and this time open the channel down to your mouth. Feel it in your mouth. Hold it there a moment, and let it back up and out your nose.

Bring more air in, and this time take it down to your throat. Feel its texture there, hold it a moment, and let it back up the channel and out your nose.

Bring it in your nostrils and this

time open up the channel from the top of your nose to your chest. Feel the air in your chest as you hold it for a moment. Let it out slowly and calmly.

Bring in more air and let it swirl around the channel and move down to your stomach, opening up the channel all the way down. Hold it at your stomach for a moment, feeling its temperature and texture, and let it back up the channel and out your nose. Feel the channel opening up, becoming more real for you, as the air molds and forms it and loosens up your body between the top of your nose and your stomach.

Inhale again and let the air gently flow down to your genitals. Feel the channel opening up this last section . . . and now running from the top of your nose all the way down to your genitals. Hold the air at your genitals for a moment and see how that feels. And then let it up slowly, and out the top of the channel.

See if you are any more aware of your body, if you have a sense of this channel now being open and providing relaxation and energy for you.

Love Mantra

Sit or lie in a relaxed position. Relieve any tension in your body by shifting position. Take a deep breath and let it out slowly. Silently finish the sentence, "Right now, my body feels ———."

Take a breath and imagine that you are filling your body with all the love that exists in the universe. As you release the breath, imagine that you are sending out all your love to the universe. Continue breathing this way for several minutes. Breathing in love, breathing out love.

Imagine that in the center of your body there's a core of love. Each time you breathe in, that core shines more brightly. Each breath you take increases the brightness of your core of love. Visualize this in any way you like, as you breathe in and out.

Next, imagine that each breath you inhale brings the energy in your love core up your body, and each breath you release moves it back down to the core at the center of your body. Breathe in and lift the love energy up, breathe out and let it sink back down. Do this for a few minutes.

Now, imagine that each time you breathe in you lift the core love energy up your body, and each time you exhale, it goes down your body, past the center, and down through your genitals and into your legs and feet. So that now when you breathe in, that love energy will rise up the entire length of your body, and when you breathe out it will flow down the entire length of your body—all the time energizing and relaxing and creating a loving feeling throughout your body. Practice this for a few moments.

Finally, each time you exhale, sending the love energy down your body, silently say the word "love" to yourself, while still visualizing the flow up and down. As you continue, let that silent repetition become an audible murmur, and then a loud chant.

Heart Mantra

Lie down and imagine your heart as if it were tightly contained, shut off from the rest of you and other people by any means you can visualize— perhaps chains, or a box, or a sack, or a glass cylinder. See how this feels for you. After a few moments, feel yourself yearning for your heart to be free and open. And then allow it to happen: feel your heart opening up and becoming free.

Place your hand over your heart— your right hand unless you are left-handed. Feel the beating of your free heart. Allow this surging life-force rhythm to relax you. Tune in to the tempo; imagine it sending its signals all through your body.

Next, keeping your one hand over your heart, and continuing to feel its beat, place your other hand over your genitals. Feel their warmth as you feel the beat of your heart. Realize they are connected. That the blood that warms your genitals is being pumped down from your heart. That the freeing of your heart also frees your genitals. Allow the beat of your heart to continue to be a mantra, or meditative guiding sound.

Realize that you are now open and vulnerable, and check out how you feel about that. That you are now connected, with the energy flowing between your heart and genitals, your hands gently resting over both organs. Check out how you feel about that. Understand that you can close off your heart at any point, put it back into its containment. Understand that you can break the connection whenever you wish, separating your heart and your genitals. Do you want to do this? Enjoy whatever you are feeling for as long as you want to feel it.

3

FLOWING FREELY

Flow is a process that is becoming more clearly defined as psychologists and social scientists explore positive psychological and physiological experiences. Transcendental Sex is aimed at creating a flow effect in all sexual activity. The foremost researcher looking into flow is Dr. Mihaly Csikszentmihalyi, a psychologist at the University of Chicago, who is universally known, for obvious reasons, as Dr. C. He describes flow as a complete immersion in what we are doing, so that we lose a conscious sense of ourselves and of time, and gain a heightened awareness of our physical involvement in whatever we are doing. People in flow find, among other benefits, that it greatly enhances concentration, generates an ecstatic feeling that everything is going just right, creates a sense of being lost in whatever they are doing, and sharpens clarity of perception. A flowing sexual experience, then, is one in which you automatically know you are doing it perfectly and have a sort of internal sense that it is going exactly right. According to Dr. C., flow can make a person feel an almost Godlike sense of control, of being in charge of the situation and on top of the world. This feeling is very similar to those described in deep meditative states, which indeed could also be called flowing.

As with meditation, when you bring flow into your sexual interaction, it not only greatly expands and enhances the experience, but the sexuality itself becomes a generator of flow. You can use meditation to increase the flow, and by flowing, you increase the meditative aspects of your sexual relating.

Preventing the Flow

Only you can prevent yourself from flowing freely in your sexual experiencing, in your sensual exploring. By hanging on to old beliefs, negative thought patterns, and parental conditioning, people inhibit their natural functioning and prohibit the full emergence of their sensual potential. You are entitled to certain sexual freedoms:

The freedom to feel.
The freedom to be vulnerable.
The freedom to shut off your mind and get into your body.
The freedom to choose innovation or comfortable familiarity.
The freedom to move away from goal orientation.
The freedom to take a full measure of pleasure for yourself.

The freedom to take charge of your own satisfaction.
The freedom to be active or passive.
The freedom to savor each moment and each sensory awareness.

And you can probably come up with many more of your own. Try filling in the blank with as many answers as you can think up:

During sex, I am free to _____.

Can you begin to see some of the ways in which you hold yourself back? Before we experience the exercises and suggestions aimed at helping your sexual flow, let's look at some of the obstacles to healthy functioning.

Sex as Evil, Dirty, and Disgusting

There is a part of each of us that responds to sex in negative ways, based on societal and parental role models and admonitions. In conducting a number of sexuality workshops, I've noticed no one, out of thousands of participants, who didn't discover *some* sexual hang-up after exploring his or her attitudes and beliefs. What is a sexual hang-up? It's anything that the thought of doing creates anxiety or discomfort or fear. You can always *choose* not to do something, but if that choice is dictated by your inability to do it, it really isn't a choice at all. If you believe sex is dirty, that sex is something that should be hidden away, always done in the dark, never discussed, then your sexual beliefs would probably be getting in the way of your being the wonderful lover you could become. Most of us have had some negative conditioning, usually from parents, in the form of admonitions about sex and our bodily functions. Some of these statements were like giant billboards placed in our minds, flashing messages such as:

"Don't touch your genitals, they are not to be played with or explored!"
"Cover your body, it's something to be ashamed of!"
"Don't touch members of the opposite sex, that's evil!"
"Don't touch members of the same sex, that's worse!"
"Sexual thoughts or feelings are horrible and unnatural!"
"Don't talk or ask questions about sex!"
"If it feels good, it's probably bad!"
"The stork brought you, so don't believe that disgusting story!"

Any of the above sound familiar? Even though you may not accept such statements as true now, chances are some of them are still inhibiting your sexual behavior to some extent. If most of your sexual activity is done in the dark, for example, you may be responding to old conditioning that said sex was something that had to be done behind closed doors, hidden from sight. Even though you may not believe that now, you could have developed this "habit" of making love only in the dark as a direct result of your emotional response to that old message. While there is nothing wrong with sex in the dark (and in flowing freely you may choose to turn the lights out), if you turn lights out because having them on makes you nervous or uncomfortable, you are the victim of a negative emotional stimulus. Just understanding the reason you feel more comfortable with the lights off may help you overcome this particular hang-up and take you to an emotional freeing that will allow you to let go and flow, with or without the lights on. It might be useful for you to explore any specific antiflow messages you got from your parents or others in your life. Sometimes this can lead to an awareness that will open up much in the way of emotional material. If you feel you can't handle this once you become aware of it, you could choose to seek professional help. I suggested this to one young woman in one of my sexual awareness groups. She was discussing, along with others in her small group, how she first heard about sex. Her mother said to her, "It's about time you learned the facts of life. You know what a boy uses to go to the bathroom with?" The little eleven-year-old girl reluctantly admitted that she did know. Her mother then continued, "Well, to make babies, a boy sticks that into where you go to the bathroom." The little girl said, "That's disgusting!" And her mother responded by saying, "That's right." Is it any wonder that as a lovely young woman, she had some sexual problems? But before talking with the group, she had never connected that specific episode with her problems. Once she had made that connection she was ready to work on it further, and a few months with a good sex therapist had her functioning as a normal and healthy woman.

Sexual Self-Stereotypes

Sexual stereotypes about ourselves are myths or general statements that have the effect of limiting our sexual exploration. They usually have to do with beliefs we have about things we've never tried, or feelings about some past performance that we allow to color all our future activity. They include such statements as:

"I am an average lover."
"I can't have an orgasm."
"I couldn't possibly get into Transcendental Sex."
"I can only enjoy sex in the morning."
"I can only respond to women with big breasts."
"I need to have a few drinks before making love."
"I can have sex only once a night."
"I couldn't handle a man with a big penis."
"I can't really satisfy a woman with a strong sex drive."
"Sex robs me of my strength and wears me out."
"As I get older, my sexual desire goes down."
"I can't have sex with someone I don't love."

"Sex during menstruation is horrible and unsatisfying."
"Oral sex is perverted."
"Anal intercourse is filthy and unpleasant."

If any of these statements are ones you could make or have made, realize that you are basing your feeling on past results, or on old beliefs. For example, you may feel like dozing for a short while after sex. This is true and normal for a lot of people. But many people say they feel more energized than ever after that little nap. To say that sex tires you out and saps your strength is therefore very limiting, since it may merely be relaxing you and allowing you to build up increased energy.

The problem is complicated by the fact that what we believe often affects what our bodies allow us to experience. If, for instance, you believe oral sex is a sick act, you will tense your muscles whenever the subject comes up. You can then accurately state that oral sex causes an unpleasant reaction in your body and assume that actually performing it would be even worse. Obviously, such an attitude would prevent the enjoyment of oral sex, or even allowing yourself to discover objectively whether or not you really like it.

Rigid Gender Beliefs

Transcendental Sex is only possible with the complete liberation of the mind from gender role stereotypes. These also involve myths and statements such as:

"Men should be aggressive, women passive."
"Men have larger sexual appetites than women."
"Women don't really enjoy sex."
"It's harder for a woman to have an orgasm than for a man."
"Men will suffer if they get aroused and aren't immediately satisfied."

"Nice girls don't do it."
"A man will lose respect for you if you give in."
"Men like their sex rough and athletic."
"Women like their sex soft and gentle."
"A woman always says 'no' even when she wants sex."
"A man is a sexual failure if he can't give a woman an orgasm."
"A woman is a sexual failure if she can't arouse a man."
"You have to tell women that you love them."
"You have to tell men you had an orgasm."

Such stereotyped beliefs create separation between the sexes and dehumanize the relationships between men and women. The truth is that men and women are more similar than not in their sexual needs, desires, and capacities. Such gender role attitudes prevent men and women from reaching their full sexual potential.

Fantasy Fears

In a sense, all fears are fantasies, since they mostly concern something that hasn't happened yet. To some extent, when making love, we all have some feelings of personal insecurity, some fear of failure or rejection. This is natural and not a major problem unless we allow it to prevent us from learning and growing and taking the risks necessary for a healthy sex life. If you ever get to a point where not being turned down or not disappointing the other person becomes more important than getting what you want, you may need to do some serious exploration of your attitudes in this area.

It's okay to fail once in a while. Actually, if you did it perfectly every time, you would be a very boring lover and never make any progress or learn anything new. If you'd had too strong a fear of failure as an infant when learning to walk, you'd probably still be crawling around on the floor. It's a statistical fact that in the United States, where mothers are constantly trying to prevent their babies from failure experiences by helping them to walk, children learn to walk at a much later age than in nations where they are left alone to explore and fail and find out for themselves. Fantasy fears have caused many people to arrest their evolution as flowing, free adults. Many are still crawling around on the floor in their sexual development. Transcendental Sex requires two healthy, mature, sensitive, and loving people. It's important to realize that you can have some of these fears, and still move forward. You don't have to allow them to hold you back. The choice is yours. Just remember that the only people who never fail are those who don't take chances, who don't explore new things, who settle only for the old and familiar. Twenty years of sexual activity involving intercourse exclusively in the missionary man-on-top position will probably produce few "mistakes," but a lot of boredom. Being able to talk over fantasy fears with a love partner can remove their destructive force. And realizing that we *all* have them can make it that much easier to discuss them.

Goals and Payoffs

Goals and payoffs are really the antithesis of Transcendental Sex, since focusing on these gets in the way of the enjoyment of whatever is happening. The idea that sex itself is the goal in the sport of seduction, that intercourse is a reasonable payoff for being nice to someone, that orgasm is the most important and only really worthwhile event in sexual relating—all of these attitudes diminish us in some way.

There is no room for seduction in the life of a truly loving person. The idea that you can receive pleasure by coercing or enticing others into doing things they really don't want to do is childish and insensitive. Flowing sexual behavior always involves two mutually agreeable adults, both acknowledging their attraction and desire for each other. Looking at the sex act as a bull's-eye, or goalpost, or sign of success, or reaffirmation of your masculinity or femininity, reduces one of life's most tender and loving experiences to the status of a spectator sport, since any of these attitudes will prevent you from being a full participant.

Some people see sex as a payoff: "If I take you to dinner and a movie, you owe me something." Traditional gender roles have usually placed the man in the position of payee versus the woman payer. It reduces the interaction to a contest: "How much can I get out of you without having to pay off in sex?" "How little can I give and still get sex?" It's impossible to enjoy sex fully under these conditions, as you're always too busy keeping score. A more subtle and possibly more destructive attitude is to see sex as a payoff for affection and commitment: "If I love you and take care of you, will you have sex with me?" In the Victorian era, and unfortunately it's still with us in some respect, there was the attitude that marriage was a bargain in which the man offered to support and take care of the woman in return for sexual favors, which the woman wasn't really supposed to enjoy. This form of legalized prostitution demeaned both the man and woman, and often destroyed any opportunity they might have had for a fulfilling sexual life.

The Big O

I remember appearing on a popular talk show called "California Girls" in San Francisco. I was amazed at how many women called in with questions about orgasm. In order not to offend the Federal Communications Commission, instead of using the word *orgasm,* we called it "the Big O." This is indicative of the fadlike status of orgasm in our culture. Along with the realization that women can really enjoy sex came devotion to the concept that good sex is always topped off with a simultaneously achieved orgasm. Unsuccessful effort at achieving this goal led to much frustration and a sense of failure in sexual relationships. More recently, the fad has been multiple orgasms, with the assumption being that since a woman can have multiple orgasms, *every* sex act must be focused on producing this result. I remember one woman in one of my sexuality groups whose husband insisted on giving her more than one orgasm, even though she was perfectly satisfied with one and usually did not enjoy a second or third, especially after his frenetic efforts at making her have them. He had thus made *her* multiple orgasms *his* goal, his proof that he was a satisfying lover. I am almost afraid to imagine what will happen with popularization of the new awareness that men also are capable of multiple orgasms—a notion resulting from our recent understanding that ejaculation is not necessarily orgasm, that the male is capable of an orgasm without ejaculating. Orgasm is a total body experience, involving increased respiration and heart rate, muscular tension, urethral and anal contractions, and a change in brain wave patterns. The important factor here, however, is that it is the subjective experience that determines how good sex is for you, not how many orgasms you have. Your one orgasm may be more satisfying for you than someone else's half dozen. When you reduce sexual performance to a statistical orgasm count, you remove all of the love and caring and flow. A number of sex researchers have expressed concern over publication of the work being done by Dr. Mina Robbins of California State University and Dr. Gordon Jensen of the University of California, who have recorded sequential multiple orgasms in males between the ages of twenty-five and fifty-five. The researchers fear this will set off a new wave of goal orientation by sexual athletes determined to set new records. Dr. Herbert Otto and Roberta Otto, in their important book, *Total Sex,* give the best reason for avoiding result-centered sexual behavior: that it gets in the way of "letting it happen organically and in its own good time, spontaneously, out of its own inner rhythm and development."

Orgasm is a release of built-up sexual energy. The building up of that energy takes longer than its release. Therefore, the more pleasure one can have during the building-up process, the more pleasurable the entire experience. Orgasm is at best a total body/mind happening, a complete release. If what precedes it is used merely as a vehicle to rush toward that release, without absorbing every possible sensual pleasure, then the final result will be less than satisfying. If you stroke your partner's thighs and your mind is firmly focused on an anticipated orgasm, you will not receive the sensory input from that particular caress, and the total event will be less than it could be. As in all interpersonal interaction, the presence of expectations, whether positive or negative, interrupts the natural momentum of sensual and sexual activity. You cannot tune in to what is happening at a given moment between you and another person when you are paying attention to either memory or anticipation.

Habitual Limitations

Here's another area that can severely hold back your sexual potential. Sex habits limit your freedom of choice. You cannot freely choose to experience a habit, since habitual behavior is behavior you are not usually aware of. Once you become aware of it, it is no longer a habit but something you are choosing to do. For instance, if you always stroke your partner's buttocks prior to having intercourse, and this has become such rigid behavior that you do it automatically, then you are not freely choosing to do it. Once you become aware of a habit, you can choose to keep doing it, modify it, or eliminate it.

It is useful to explore your own individual habits and patterns, for these can create monotony, one of the prime enemies of Transcendental Sex. Some habits and patterns identified by participants in my sexual awareness groups:

> The same partner always initiating sexual activity.
> Sexual activity in the same place at the same time of day.
> Following the same progression of foreplay.

> Playing music every time you make love.
> Always taking a shower before sex.
> Always having sex in bed.
> Always making noise during sex.
> Always being quiet during sex.
> Always building the tempo from slow to fast movements.
> Always having the same partner grasp and insert the penis.
> Always having orgasm in the same male-female order.
> Always starting sexual activity in the nude.

There is nothing wrong with doing any of these things once in a while, but if you have so deadened your sensitivity that you do any of them all the time in monotonous regularity, then you are severely limiting the possibilities.

There is a good chance you can identify some of your own sexual habits if you sit down and think about it. For instance, you may always choose to sleep on the same side of the bed. Almost everyone has a favorite side of the bed, one on which he or she feels most comfortable. If you always end up on the same side of your partner, however, there's a good chance part of your partner's body is being touch-neglected. If you are on the left side of your partner, there's no way you could be paying as much attention to your partner's right side. Also, this habit often involves manipulation, since both partners may prefer the same side and one would then have to submit to the other. After becoming aware of your own rigidity, even if you still most often choose that favorite side of the bed, it will now be done as a conscious choice, and you'll be your own emotional master rather than a slave to habit.

One of the factors that may lead to sexual habits and patterns is the refusal of one or both partners to recognize that two unique individuals are involved. Some people tend to do the same things with every sex partner they have ever had, not taking this uniqueness into account, not checking out what really feels good for and with this person. For instance, if you have had a long relationship with one sexual partner, you probably have had a favorite sexual position with that person. If you continue to choose that position most frequently with a new partner, you are not responding to the unique and individual characteristics of the new partner. Your former favorite position may not feel as good with this new person, and you severely limit the potential of that relationship if you insist on favoring it, rather than checking out what feels good and experimenting until you feel the relative differences and similarities of your two bodies and how they fit together. One way to avoid destructive habits is to relate to a sex partner as a new person, with new possibilities that require exploration.

Of course, not all habits are bad, but it is useful and important to recognize them. And there's nothing wrong in enjoying the old and familiar and comfortable, as long as you do it freely and with an awareness of alternatives. In fact, always having to do something new can also become a destructive habit. Routine isn't bad if it's routine you honestly enjoy, and as long as it's interspersed with variety and spontaneity.

Verbal Repression

Another major obstacle on the road to flowing freely is being unwilling to discuss openly your sexual feelings and preferences with a partner or to ask for what you want. A primary reason for avoiding this kind of forthright communication is the fear that it will be unacceptable to the other person. And this may stem from an inner feeling or belief that natural sexual inclinations are unhealthy or abnormal. A good way to begin to overcome this limitation is to discuss openly with your partner your fears and fantasies and sexual history. Verbal repression, fear of being rejected or embarrassed, and refusing to ask for what you want all lead to physical repression as well. You cannot have a flowing sexual connection when merely talking about it makes you anxious.

If you find it hard to ask for what you want, it may help to look at why you find it hard. Is it because you don't want to impose yourself on another person?

Is it because you feel you don't deserve to get what you want? Is it because you expect the other person to read your mind and give you what you want without your asking for it? Are you afraid you will hurt the other person's feelings by implying you're not satisfied? Or are you just shy? All the meditation and sexual performing in the world can't give you what you want if you can't ask for it. Asking for something you'd like your partner to do for you sexually is something most people have difficulty doing. This stems from our conditioning that sex shouldn't be talked about, and certainly shouldn't be discussed with the actual or potential sex partner. It's supposed to just happen. Some people call this flowing. It's not flowing at all, it's wishful thinking. Being able to communicate desires and feelings deeply is the only way to become a flowing sexual partner. And it doesn't always have to be verbal communication. Being able to take your partner's hand and place it somewhere you would like it to be can enhance the natural flow. Look at it this way: wouldn't you like to know what gives your partner particular pleasure? And can you accept the fact that your partner would appreciate the same information from you?

A Lovely Bunch of Hang-ups

Reading this chapter up to this point, one could get the idea that we are all hopelessly hung up in our sexual behavior, and that the chances for normal sexual functioning, let alone Transcendental Sex, are almost nonexistent. The exciting and wonderful truth is that once you accept the fact that you are human and have normal fears and hang-ups, you can begin discarding the things that prevent you from flowing freely. You might see sex as dirty, evil, and disgusting, or adhere to any number of sexual stereotypes and rigid gender roles, or feel fantasy fears, or be goal oriented, or limit yourself to habit, or repress verbal communication. And none of that has to prevent you from experiencing Transcendental Sex, *if* you understand that right now you can make a choice to open up and do it all differently. A room can be dark for a thousand years, but as soon as you light one candle it isn't dark anymore. The same is true for you. As soon as you light the light of awareness, you are ready to move forward.

Once you recognize those obstacles in your path, you can step around them. Once you acknowledge your liabilities, you can focus all your attention on your many assets. The reality is that it doesn't take a special, superhuman person to perform Transcendental Sex. All it takes is someone who is alive and willing to discover his or her hidden potential, willing to experiment with some satisfying new behavior, willing to be sensitive to his or her own needs and those of a partner.

Belief versus Flow

Whatever you believe about sex and your own sexual potential, recognize this truth: It ain't necessarily so! The focus throughout this book is on experience, on checking out what happens when you do something—not what you believe will happen, but what *actually* happens. There is a certain organic order to things, a certain natural momentum. Belief can interfere with this. If, for instance, you believe a certain sexual act will be unpleasant, and you have never tried it, that belief will modify your behavior and prevent you from healthy experimentation. It's normal to have preconceptions, but destructive to allow them to interfere with the reality of experience. A lot of the aforementioned hang-ups and barriers have to do with your belief system. Remember this: Any beliefs you hold on to without experience to back them up have had to have come from other people. You are clinging to a lot of other people's beliefs, and if you don't check them against your own experience, if you allow them to prevent your own experience, you may as well be a mechanical, programmed robot, without mind, imagination, or feelings.

Freeing the Body/Mind

At any given moment, you are as free as you choose to be. Once you recognize any mental, emotional, and physical limitations, you can stuff them all into an imaginary box and toss them on the trash pile. By focusing on your awareness on a moment-to-moment basis, you activate your natural flowing energies and become the perfect lover you have always been capable of becoming. The exercises coming up are designed to help facilitate this letting go of mind and body. Most of them involve a partner, who should be equally willing to explore and let go. Some of the exercises are sexual in nature, focusing on the genitals; others are primarily sensual in nature, focusing on awareness in other body parts or throughout the body. As you practice the art of Transcendental Sex, these distinctions will become blurred, and all your loving interaction will be sensual/sexual, whether or not it specifically involves intercourse or sexual release. Don't overdo the exercises. Tune in to your body signals, and trust their messages. If a certain position or exercise is tiring your body, relax and then move on to something else. One way to view your reaching out to your partner is to imagine that he or she is a newborn baby, needing and wanting to be touched, but so very gently.

The exercises are guidelines, tools to help you move into new awarenesses and new ways of sharing. Feel free to modify them, to invent your own, to enjoy those that fit you and your partner, and to discard those that don't. If you want to follow some of the more meditative, sensual experiences with vigorous and uninhibited sex, by all means do so. Do what feels right *when* it feels right and you cannot go wrong. Getting away from goal orientation also means not having specific goals while you are actually experimenting. Ask yourself now, before trying out any of the exercises, "Do I have any expectations?" If you do, see if you can't also let those go, and just be.

Self-Touching

In all the years you've lived with your body, there's a very good chance that you have never really given yourself time to know it. You cannot be a sensitive lover without being a sensitive person, and you are the best person on whom to practice sensitivity. Usually the best way to please another person is to do something that would give you pleasure if it were done for you. Trying out various strokes and caresses on yourself is a way to help you tune in to what feels good, and it gives you a sense of what the other person is feeling as you give him or her pleasure. When you give to another as you would give to yourself, you create a spiritual connection, a special bond between you, and the pleasure and the flowing increase proportionately.

With one finger of one hand, slowly begin tracing over all the parts of your body you can reach. Be aware of how your body feels to your finger and how your finger feels to your body. Ask yourself which parts feel best getting touched, and find out whether there are any that feel especially good but haven't been getting touched during your sexual activity.

When you have finished exploring your body in this way, use both hands tenderly to caress wherever you can reach with comfort. Use a calming stroke, as if you were making an effort to soothe and relax yourself. Be aware of your internal attitude as you continue this personal exploration. Ask yourself the following questions:

> *Am I relaxed?*
> *Am I enjoying this experience?*
> *Do I believe I can give myself pleasure?*
> *Do I believe that this is a healthy and natural thing to do for myself?*

Take your earlobe between the thumb and forefinger and gently massage it, being aware of its flexibility and its texture and even its temperature. Also be aware of how this feels and whether you think it would feel good to have another person do this for you, or to do it for another person.

Play with your knee. Get in there and massage around the bone, exploring the indentations and the various ways in which you can move the skin and muscle around.

With the tips of your fingers, explore your buttocks. Push in hard and vibrate the fingers rapidly to tone up this area. Gently caress the surface of the skin. Be aware of the differences between these two types of touch.

Play with your feet. Bend your toes. Press your thumbs into the soles of your feet, running them down the length from toe to heel. Run one finger between your toes. Massage your ankles. Bend and flex the foot with your hands. Pull your big toes with your hands. For thousands of years, various cultures have believed that the big toe is connected to sexual energy. Can you feel any connection?

Rest one hand lightly on your genitals. Feel the warmth and weight of the hand. Explore your genitals. Don't try to arouse yourself. If that happens, it's okay, but merely see what you can discover about the texture and flexibility and warmth and feel of your genitals.

See if you can explore the difference between touching your genitals merely to explore the touch sensations, and touching to arouse yourself. First, just touch for a few moments. Then, caress in a way you find arousing.

Beginning Ritual

Sit in comfortable position, facing each other, knees touching, looking into each other's eyes. Rest your hands softly on your own genitals, feeling the warmth. One at a time, each partner says the following, maintaining eye contact:

I AM HERE WITH YOU. MY MIND IS HERE. MY BODY IS HERE. MY EMOTIONS ARE HERE. OF ALL THE UNIVERSE, THIS IS THE PLACE I CHOOSE TO BE, AND YOU ARE THE ONE I CHOOSE TO BE WITH. ALL THE LOVE I FEEL RIGHT NOW, I AM READY TO SHARE WITH YOU. THANK YOU FOR SHARING WITH ME, AND FOR RECEIVING WHAT I OFFER.

If these words don't feel quite right, change them to suit you and your partner. This is a moment for preparation, for separating the coming experiences from your daily routine, for quieting the mind and body, and for appreciating yourself and your partner. Understand that the sentence beginning "All the love I feel right now . . ." is a deep commitment; it says your warm feelings for each other are the underlying motivation for the following experiments.

Breathing Union

Lie on your backs, side by side, holding hands, with eyes closed. Place your free hands on your own abdomens, and feel the rise and fall. Without working too hard at it, let your breathing rhythms join and blend, so that you are breathing in synchronous harmony. You may choose to use the Seven-In/Hold-One/Seven-Out breathing format explained in chapter 2, or just allow your breathing to happen.

Continuing your breathing, move your free hands to your own genitals. Imagine that each inhalation is sending energy to your sexual center, and that each exhalation is sending that sexually charged energy throughout your body. If that imagery is difficult for you, then don't worry about it; tune in to whatever the synchronous breathing feels like for you.

Hold each other close, either lying down or sitting, in a warm, cuddling embrace. Allow yourself to feel each other's breathing, and the movements of the body that correspond to the breathing action. Again, begin to breathe in harmony, using the awareness of each other's bodies to guide you.

You may choose to alternate your breathing pattern. One partner breathes in while the other breathes out, thus forming another rhythmic connection.

The Finger Trip

One partner lies on his or her back, and the other lightly traces over the entire surface of the body with one finger. The pressure should be light, but steady and consistent. The partner doing the touching should do it very slowly, really noticing the sensations from the contact made with each small area of the other person's body. The partner lying down should just let go and feel whatever is happening. The genitals are to be treated as just another body area, not neglected, not given special attention. Wait a few minutes at the end before switching roles.

After the Finger Trip, you may choose to try the same thing with two fingers, then three, moving up to the whole hand, and perhaps even bringing in the other hand.

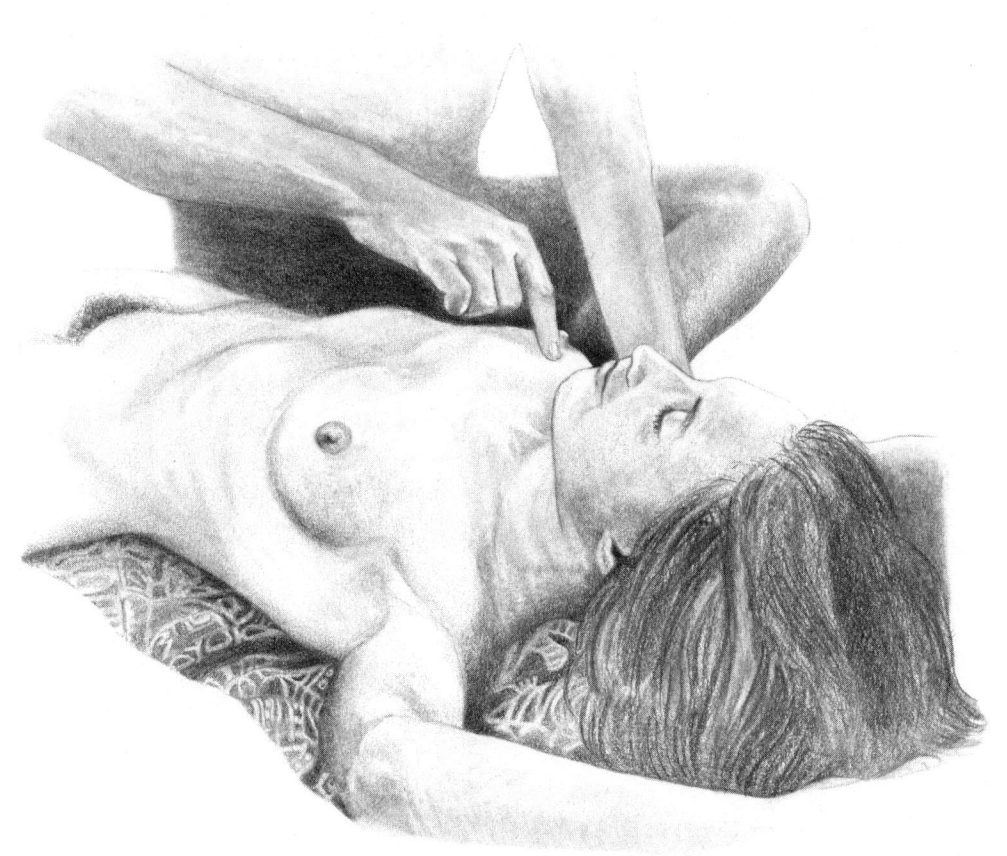

Chanting Together

Facing each other, making eye contact and holding hands, start to chant the phrase:

WE ARE ONE

Allow the volume to build slowly, and continue chanting just a little while after you first feel inclined to stop. Allow your mind to disengage during the chanting, so that the words become meaningless. Allow your voice to rise and fall in pitch, without sinking into a dull monotone.

After the chanting, just be still for a few moments.

Next, in a warm embrace, begin slowly chanting the word:

LOVE

This time, allow the tempo to build, but see if you can't be in touch with all the love you feel for yourself and for your partner. Allow the chant to express this for a few moments, and then let go of the feeling and the meaning, and let your mind disengage.

The Touching Connection

Sit facing your partner. You may cross your legs in the lotus position, or take any other sitting position that feels comfortable. One partner may sit with legs straight out, resting over the other partner's legs. It is important that you feel relaxed and are not straining any muscles or creating any tension that can distract. The first step is merely to look at each other. Examine each other's bodies with your eyes. You are silent, but feel free to express feelings to each other with your eyes and facial expressions. Close your eyes after you feel you've communicated some sense of yourselves to each other. Now your partner places both hands on your cheeks and just lets them rest there, feeling the warmth and texture of the skin. You remain motionless, perhaps with the hands resting on the knees, palms up in a meditative position. Your partner's hands begin to move gently, exploring and caressing your face and head, your ears, the top of your head, and the back of your neck. Very slowly the hands move over the entire surface of your head. Very lightly they touch the skin. You focus on the sensations of the touching. Thoughts may come in to distract. Thoughts, for example, about what you are going to do when your turn comes to touch. Allow those thoughts to flow by. Don't

hold on to them; don't fight them. Silently say to them, "Not now," for you can always get back to the thoughts, but you cannot ever recapture this actual experience. After a total exploration of the face and head, your partner slowly removes his or her hands, so slowly that it may be difficult to feel when they actually leave the surface of the skin. Both of you stay quiet and motionless for a minute or so. Then roles are switched, again starting with hands on the cheeks. Again, when this is finished, a moment of quiet reflection. Still no talking between partners.

The first partner then slowly begins to explore the other's shoulders and arms. Another quiet reflective moment after withdrawal, and roles are again switched. Another quiet period when this is finished.

Both partners now start to touch each other, slowly and simultaneously, wherever they wish, focusing on each patch of skin as a separate entity without paying attention to what it is or where it is located. You may choose to leave the genitals off limits during this initial exploration, or just touch them as if they were any other part of the body, without specific sexual significance. You should decide whether they are to be included before starting the exercise. From time to time throughout the touching, you may find yourself becoming sexually aroused. This is natural. It feels good. Enjoy it. And be aware that your whole body is feeling good, not just your genitals. Part of the flow is back and forth from sensuality to sexuality. The important thing is not to attempt to sexually arouse. Whatever happens, happens. If you do get aroused, do not interrupt the experience to have sex or an orgasm. You will not suffer if you do not have immediate sexual release. This is a cultural myth, and it is time to discard it. It gets in the way of a lot of sensual pleasure.

You may continue touching as

long as you wish. There is, however, one final structured part of the connection that is important. When you have finished your touching, come together in an embrace, and remain absolutely still together for at least five minutes. This will allow you to feel each other's warmth and energy, and give you time to absorb the experience.

You may then choose to talk about your feelings and individual experiences. After this, you may choose to make love. This particular exploration is over, so whatever you do next will not detract from it or dilute it. You may find, however, that you both feel very physically satisfied and are quite content just to be together or even to end your interaction and go your separate ways. Let each other know how you feel and what you want. Sometimes our programming and conditioned belief systems say to us that it is time for sex, but we may feel very satisfied without it. If you are not used to feeling this kind of satisfaction, it can be a most valuable lesson for you. But you have not failed any meditative standard if you happen to be aroused and want to release that sexual energy. Accept yourself as a sexual being and enjoy that part of you! Enjoy whatever happens, wherever your flowing takes you.

The Ear Exploration

This is an exercise in which we pay specific attention to one of the most sensitive of all body parts, your ears.

One partner is behind the other, either standing or sitting. The partner in back gently takes both ears between the fingers and massages the entire outer surface; then, using the index fingers, traces around the lobe, in a circular pattern, finally inserting the fingers into the earhole just enough to shut off a good bit of the audible sounds. The fingers remain in the ears for about thirty seconds, and then are slowly withdrawn, as the back of the ear is firmly massaged with one or two fingers.

Switch roles and repeat the exercise.

Genital Contact

Both partners lie on their backs, with genitals touching and one partner's legs over the other's legs. Your feet are under your partner's armpits.

Experiment so that this becomes a cozy position. Perhaps you'll want to raise your knees to increase comfort. The idea is to have your genitals touching, but in a position in which sex would not be possible. Keeping your feet under the arms creates a certain warmth and allows the body heat and energy to remain flowing between you. You may want to stroke your partner's legs while in this posture.

Tell each other how this feels for you.

Genital Stroking

One of the purposes of Transcendental Sex is to bring you to a point where your entire skin surface is erogenous and as sexually sensitive as your genitals are now. This may seem farfetched, but seeing it as one direction to take can lead you to the realization that your brain is your only real erogenous zone. You get aroused by the touching of your genitals primarily because you expect to. While there are physiological sensations that are most pleasing from genital touching and stroking, a major proportion of the effect of this touching is based on your preconceptions, which in turn are based on memory, conditioning, and anticipation. This exercise is designed to provide you with more information about this phenomenon, and to use genital touching and stroking as a new tool for awareness.

Lie or sit in a comfortable position. Decide which partner will go first. This partner then slowly begins to rest his or her hand on the other's genitals, allowing the full weight of the hand to be felt very gradually. Slowly begin stroking. Rather than aiming at arousing your partner, stroke from a perspective of caring for this other human being, and caring for this particular part of the body. See this as person-to-person interaction, and not just as hand-to-

genital contact. After stroking for several minutes, stop. Slowly lift the hand. Both partners should close eyes at this point if they have not already done so. Just sit quietly and absorb the sensations. In a minute or two, switch roles.

After this sequence, sit quietly for a couple of minutes. Then begin to stroke each other's genitals simultaneously. Do this for three or four minutes. All the stroking is very gentle, very caring.

Note: *It is important to emphasize again that it is all right to become aroused during this experience. In fact, it's even okay to go on and have sex and an orgasm. We are exploring alternative attitudes and increased sensitivity, not necessarily alternative results. If you are really in a meditative state of mind, you will be receptive to whatever happens.*

You will eventually, at your own pace, discover that genital stroking can be very pleasant even without moving to direct sexual contact or to immediate sexual release. You can stroke and even arouse each other, and then slow down and stop a number of times without feeling frustrated. This frees you physically and emotionally. It frees you, for example, to touch genitals at various times in various situations where sexual release may not be possible.

Couples often avoid each other's genitals except immediately prior to intercourse, and this is a shame. Your genitals need as much non-sexual stroking as the rest of your body. They are not separate entities, but an integral part of your entire physiological system. You may be limited in the number of times you can or want to achieve sexual release in any given time period. But during that same time period, you can be stroked and caressed in unlimited loving interaction. And it feels so good!

Varying Perspectives

If there are any number of sexual positions, there are even more sensual positions, and you may have been limiting your exploration in this area. Play with arranging your bodies in different poses that enable you to focus on new touch sensations.

One position, which I call the Enclosure, has one partner reclining against the other, enclosed by arms and legs. The reclining partner is in front of the other, with the back against the rear partner's chest and abdomen. This creates a warm sense of comfort, and enables you to stroke each other in new ways, from a new perspective.

Another switch in perspective comes when you lie foot to head. This enables you to play with each other's legs and feet, and increase sensitivity to each other's body. It also might be a unique experience for you to fall asleep this way. I've watched my Siamese cats sleep together in so many fascinating positions, and often thought that we human beings are really restricted in our sleeping-together postures.

Lying on your backs with the soles of your feet touching can allow you to play with balancing your feet together, putting pressure against your partner's feet, and allowing this to lift the feet. You can slide closer together, moving the feet up your partner's legs, slowly approaching the genitals.

Body-Parts Contact

This is an adventure in making contact with your partner in some ways you may not have explored before. The idea is to focus on how these contact points feel. You can play with this and have fun with it.

Make contact between one of your partner's arms and one of yours. Allow the entire lengths of the arms to touch. Be aware of how your arm feels and how your partner's arm feels to you.

Make contact by touching your chins and nothing else.

Make buttocks to buttocks contact.

Touch the bottoms of your feet together.

Touch ears together.
Chest to chest.
Leg to leg.
Touch the tops of your heads.

Each contact should last about a minute and be done silently. You can choose to keep your eyes open or closed.

After you have finished, hold each other in a comfortable position and share your feelings about this experiment.

You can really play with this. You may touch one part of your body to another part of your partner's body—for instance, chin to chest.

4
SHARING ENERGY

Sex is energy, and sexual interaction is the building up and eventual release of that energy. It may be released in orgasm or it may be released within the bodies of the man and woman as sexual arousal is allowed to subside. Either event can be an energizing and healthy one, provided the motivation is healthy. If, however, sexual release is a desperately sought-after goal or is used to control another person or vent hostility, a harmful and emotionally damaging effect results. The same is true if sexual release is avoided out of fear, anger, or manipulation. In Eastern philosophy, it is taught that there is a cosmic or universal energy or life force, and that this is divided into two parts, one residing in the male, the other in the female. Thus sexual union is seen as the bringing back together of this powerful universal force. The Chinese call the female energy *yin,* and the male energy *yang.* In Hindu and Tantric tradition, the female is *shakti,* and the male is *shiva.* A number of Western scientists have affirmed that there is some sort of bioelectrical energy in the human body and that there is a difference between male and female energy. Though research is limited in this area, there are strong indications that something special happens when two highly compatible people of the opposite sex join in sensual or sexual activity. And you've no doubt heard the expression "There was electricity in the air" used to describe the meeting of a man and a woman. This may be much more than a metaphor.

Sexual energy is merely a manifestation of our basic life energy, and as such is most fully appreciated as a part of the totality of our being. If the only time you feel awake and alive is during sexual activity, then you may be missing the point. If you are dull, lethargic, and uninterested in life, you're not going to be a very sensitive or exciting lover. With a strong sense of vitality, you will have an abundance of energy to share with your love partner. All sensual and sexual relating is, after all, the sharing of energy.

Some cultures believe that women are the senders and men the receivers of the energy exchange; others teach that the opposite is true. In the Hindu and Tantric traditions, the woman is considered passive and magnetic, attracting the male electrical energy, absorbing it, and thus creating a reaction, a generating of power. In any event, this theorizing is purely academic, since we each possess masculine and feminine qualities and energies, in varying degrees. Each of us is a unique blend of these forces, a blend that can only relate in a unique way to that of another individual.

Not everybody is compatible in terms of energy. For instance, have you ever been attracted to a member of the opposite sex but then found that spending time with this person wore you out, depleted your energy level? Some people energize and replenish us, others deplete and drain us. And whether you attribute this to energy incompatibility or to basic personality conflict, it is important to pay attention to these signals. There is also temporary incompatibility, which happens when one or both partners are angry, inhibited, afraid, or depressed. This is not the time for a healthy exchange of loving energy. Common sense should dictate this, but we sometimes allow erotic passion to override our natural sense of timing.

Intermingling Auras

Many people believe that the body is surrounded by an energy field—often called the *aura*—extending several inches out from the skin surface. There is even some scientific evidence to back this up, in the form of Kirlian photography, a process that seems to show electrical energy emanating from the body. Kirlian photographs taken of healers in the process of laying their hands on patients have shown this energy leaving the hands of the healer and apparently going into the body of the patient. Auras come in many colors, and some people seem to be able to see colorful energy fields surrounding the body. For the purposes of this book, it doesn't really matter whether you accept all this or not. If, however, you will at least imagine that you do have a unique aura that surrounds your body, you can see that any sensual or sexual activity would involve this aura, and, in fact, your aura would intermingle and connect with that of your partner. This blending of energies can be a very potent experience, both physically and emotionally. The more sensitive you become to your own energy level and potential, the more sensitive you will become to a partner's unique energy field.

This life force, or creative energy, when manifested as sexual energy, can be either positive or negative, as can all energy. It may be put to good or bad use, generated by healthy or unhealthy motivation. In addition to the positive Tantric tradition in Tibet, for example, there used to be sects of negative practitioners who used sexual energy to enslave, manipulate, and degrade others. What you have in your heart will have a lot to do with how you and your partner experience the energy exchange.

There is also, of course, a purely physiological buildup of tension during the arousal period, and this creates its own energy, particularly at the moment of release. Bernard Gunther, one of the pioneering group leaders in the human potential movement, wrote in his book *What to Do Till the Messiah Comes*:

> *tension is energy*
> *that wants to be*
>
> *love*
>
> *shared*
>
> *spent*
>
> *allowed to*
> *flow free*

The last line is an important one. We've already talked about how crucial flowing freely was to a gratifying sensual/sexual experience; it's equally important in terms of activating your full energy potential. Look at the sometimes unbelievable level of energy in a small child. I remember attending a workshop for people who taught education at the college level. To focus awareness on the tremendous energy resources of young children, the teacher had us play a game featured on a children's record, involving moving around as if we were all puppets, up and down, up and down, up and down, and dancing around the room. After a half hour of this, we were all exhausted. The instructor then told us that a child from five to eight years of age will play the game three times as long and still beg for more! There is no reason whatsoever why we shouldn't have that same level of energy in our adult lives. It gets stifled by parents and teachers, but we can choose to remove those fetters and once again have the freedom to flow. The more childlike freedom there is, the more powerful the effect of integrating the male and female energies.

The purpose of this chapter is not to explain or define this energy. It may be many years before we understand its true composition in scientific terms. If you have experienced it, you know it is there. If you have ever felt something in the air in the presence of two people in love, felt an indefinable tingle pass between you and a member of the opposite sex, or felt energized and more alive as the result of a loving experience, then you have already tuned in to this kind of energy and are ready to explore it further at an experiential, subjective level.

Noted sex therapists Drs. Claude and Dorothy Nolte, in their book, *Waking Up In Bed Together,* say, "We see the projection of warm feelings as a form of transmission of 'energy.'" In experiments performed by researchers in this area, it certainly seems that the phenomenon of energy exchange occurs most often and most sharply between two people who have built up a strong level of caring, comfort, and trust. This may be the best argument of all for a long-term relationship versus casual sexual encounters. A number of couples who are deeply in love have reported that one or both of the partners at times seem to be surrounded by a bright glow, as if electrically charged. This may not happen for you, but if it does, it is nothing to be frightened of, even if it can't be immediately explained. In any event, you have probably, at one time or another, felt yourself bathed in a warm glow of indescribable satisfaction while with a love partner. This, too, is a manifestation of the energy that passes between two lovers.

Energy is something we are still researching in the human body, and we don't yet know its exact character. It could be electromagnetic, as suggested by the Eastern philosophies, some of which see the man as sending out electricity and the woman receiving it as a powerful magnet; or it might have to do with the generation of body heat; or perhaps it's connected with the building up and final release of sexual tension. In any case, there certainly is something that a man and a woman share during sensual and sexual activity that cannot be explained in basic physical terms. So, for want of a more precise way to describe it, let us call it "energy," and see, in the upcoming exercises, whether we can actually feel it happening.

Love as Energy

Psychologist Dr. Marjorie Toomim and her scientist husband, Hershel Toomim, see love as an exchange of energy. In a paper entitled "The Experience of Love," which they delivered at the California State Psychological Convention in January 1975, they stated:

> Life is a moving energy field. It flows as we hold and let go, attach and separate, give and take, come and go. In order to fully participate in this vital, living energy flow we must be capable of experiencing acceptance, trust, caring, sensing, hearing, seeing, understanding and sharing knowledge, feeling and sharing emotions. These intangible qualities unite us with life. Love is a feeling that arises from within us. It grows only when nourished by the same qualities that are essential to participation in the flow of life. To love, as to live, requires an exchange of energy—a flow. I am aware that I feel good when I am with you. I feel life-energies flow through me when I talk to you and touch you. I feel warm and excited when I think of you. I carry an image of you with me when we are apart. I want to connect with you by sharing these perceptions, feelings and thoughts with you. As I do this, I know that I risk your misunderstanding, perhaps even your rejection. However, I trust myself. I know that I am capable of coping with frustration,

rejection and hurt feelings, and so I will communicate my feelings to you with words and with my behavior. If you are open to perceive, understand, accept and respect the thoughts and feelings I share with you, one part of the energy exchange is completed. I have experienced my own energies, used them in communicating to you, and hopefully you have taken in some of my energy—my being—by accepting my touch, my words, etc. If, now, you can communicate to me that you have received and accepted what I have offered, and if your communication is meaningful to me and accepted by me, then the energy exchange is complete. We have made a connection with each other. The connection is strengthened if, in addition to letting me know that you have accepted my thoughts and feelings, you share your awareness of your feelings toward me in a way which I can accept and find meaningful. If your thoughts and feelings are at all commensurate with mine, then our experience will be heightened. We probably will feel a surge of energy and excitement as we recognize that we are united by a bond of good feeling. At this moment, warmth flows freely between us. At this moment, we may believe we are united by a bond of love. We may say we are experiencing loving feelings.

We all feel energized and alive in a relationship where good feelings, trust, and acceptance are experienced and communicated in a way which is meaningful and acceptable. We feel energized and alive when ideas and emotions arise easily within us and are freely given, received, and returned enriched by the other's experience and expression. We feel energized and alive in a relationship in which our needs may be expressed and respected, and where enough care exists that needs are gratified. In such a relationship, we feel love. We say we are loved. Love is the feeling which is normally engendered within us when we participate in a relationship in which we are open to these qualities of being within ourselves and where these qualities are freely exchanged between ourselves and others in ways that are meaningful and satisfying.

In this segment from their paper, the Toomims have attempted to explain the essence of love. This model can certainly be applied to sexual sharing. Does it make sense for you?

Emotional Release

Holding in the emotions, whatever they may be, and refusing to share them or reveal them to your partner will greatly inhibit the energy exchange. For energy to build up in the body, the individual must be as relaxed as possible. Holding back feelings causes certain muscles to constrict and creates tension. Not the natural and desirable sexual tension, but a rigid, energy-draining muscular tension that results in dull and disappointing sex.

The more you have allowed yourself to trust your partner, the more of your emotions you are willing to share, and the more vulnerability you reveal, the more powerful and fulfilling your sexual experience will be. Creating a meditative atmosphere by using the Transcendental Sex approach will foster growth and increased ability in this area.

I particularly noted the connection between relaxation/meditation and the building up of healthy sexual energy when I was running the Biofeedback Institute in New York. I remember one session in which I was training a group of women to raise the temperature of their hands several degrees by using a form of the Primary Relaxation Experience described in chapter 2 and a temperature biofeedback unit that gave them immediate feedback of how well they were doing. This was, in effect, teaching them to control blood flow (and, by the way, it has been found to be effective treatment for migraine headaches). Dr. Elmer Green pioneered this work at the Menninger Foundation. At the end of my training session, I asked the women to report on their subjective experiences, what they actually felt happening during the session. Out of a total of ten women training, six of them reported physical sensations that reminded them of sexual stimulation, and two of the women said they felt themselves approaching orgasm. Since then, a number of people have told me that they began to have sensations of sexual arousal during relaxation inductions.

That relaxation is very much a prerequisite for the building of sexual energy is also seen in the fact that so many people so often find themselves experiencing sexual desire when they wake up in the morning, after a good night's sleep.

Trust

When we see that the energy that builds and flows between two people is enhanced by the meditative/relaxed state of consciousness, then it becomes obvious that trust plays a big part in the exchange. You have to trust someone in order to let go of any emotions you are holding back, to feel relaxed in another's presence, and to be willing to share the joyful energy you will experience with increased sensitivity and perception. You have to trust that this other person will not drain you of your energy but will be willing to share his or her energy, creating a circular effect. In my book *My Needs, Your Needs, Our Needs,* sex therapist Carole Altman described this phenomenon:

> You're totally tuned into the person with you and his feelings. Whether it be joy or pleasure, pain or orgasm, whatever the feelings being felt by the person with you, you feel them, too. What you actually feel is no beginning or end of yourself. You become circular, one with the other. Your energies are merging, and actually being transmitted as messages to each other. So that it's almost a constant round robin, with your energies, feelings, sensitivities going into him and vice versa. Finally, it's just the two of you, in a floating, spherical relationship of energy and love, joy and pleasure. Your empathy is increased so tremendously that you just understand each other. Not on an intellectual level, but on an emotional level.

Does this sound very difficult or complicated? Well, it's not. Suspend your judgment for a while about whether or not you can achieve this blissful state. Just enjoy the exercises without demanding anything specific in the way of results. Trust also means trusting yourself and your own capacity to learn and to grow.

The Energy Exercises

Some of these exercises are designed to wake you up and alert your senses, so that you and your partner may discover each other in your fully alive states. This, too, has to do with energy and the sharing thereof. See how much you can find out for yourself in these experiments. You may find yourself becoming aroused during some of them. That's okay; just deal with that in any way you want to, any way that feels right at that moment. If you repress a natural feeling or desire in order to do the exercise "the way it's supposed to be done," you are missing the whole point of this book!

And don't make heavy demands on yourself. If an exercise suggests that you feel a certain sensation, and you don't, just accept whatever you feel as what you are supposed to be feeling. Enjoy your uniqueness, and share it.

The Center of Your Being

This is a relaxation exercise focusing on energy, and you may choose to tape-record it and listen to it together, or take turns reading it to each other.

Lie on your back in a comfortable position. Allow your legs to spread out to where they feel most relaxed. Allow your hands to rest at your sides, or anywhere else you may prefer.

Now that your body is comfortable, concentrate on your breathing. Don't change it, just concentrate on it. Think about each breath as it goes in and out. Imagine you can actually see the air going in and coming out. Experience and appreciate the movement of the various muscles involved in your breathing. Continue to breathe in and out as you normally do. (Pause 20 seconds.)

When you breathe in, your body is taking in all it requires from the universe. When you breathe out, you are giving back to the universe whatever you don't need. Feel this process happening for you. Breathing in and taking from the universe its life-giving oxygen, sending back what you don't need by exhaling, so that it may nourish plants and be reprocessed by nature. Picture your entire breathing system working to fill your body with oxygen. See this oxygen delivering energy through your lungs, into your heart, into your entire bloodstream and cardiovascular system, bringing nourishment and energy down into your arms and hands and fingers, into your stomach and genitals and legs and feet, up into your shoulders and neck and face and head and hair and brain. Feel yourself as an important and vital part of the universe. Become aware of your role in the universe, of the necessity of your existence in the total scheme of things, as you breathe in and out, feeling good about sharing with the universe all that you are, all that you have. (Pause 20 seconds.)

Imagine, right next to your body, a shiny ball in a clear glass tube. As you breathe in, imagine the ball rising to the top of the glass tube. As you breathe out, imagine the ball moving back down the tube. Watch the ball as it goes up and down, keeping time with your breathing, moving up as you breathe in, moving down as you breathe out. (Pause 20 seconds.)

As your breath keeps time with the rise and fall of the ball in the tube, move them inside your body. See the ball and tube inside of you, still continuing the same movement, with the ball rising as you breathe in, and falling as you breathe out. As you breathe in, the ball moves to the top of the tube; as you breathe out, it moves down. With each breath, you relax a bit more. And, as you relax, each time you breathe in, the ball rises less than the time before. Each time you inhale, it rises to a lower spot in the tube. And each time you breathe out, the ball sinks a bit farther than it did before. Each time you exhale, it falls to a lower spot in the tube. The ball slowly sinks lower and lower, and eventually comes to rest in the pit of your stomach, just below your navel. This, many spiritual masters tell us, is the core, the center of our being, of our life force, of our energy. Take all the time you need until the shiny ball settles in the center of your being. Let your breathing relax you. Watch the ball *rising less each time, and sinking slowly toward the center, coming to rest there, just below your navel, and thus letting you know that you are completely relaxed and that all the energy you possess is focused at your center, where the ball has come to rest. Allow the ball to come to rest there. If it is there already, just enjoy whatever you are feeling. (Pause 20 seconds.)*

As the ball rests at the center of your being, you feel all your energy being focused there. You can test whether this is true for you. From this center, you can send energy to any part of your body, anywhere you'd like it to be. To start this process, send some energy out to your fingertips. Very slowly, send the energy out from the center of your being and up toward your shoulder. Feel it as it moves through your stomach and chest. Let yourself be aware of the energy as it moves across your shoulder and begins to flow down along your arm and into one of your hands. Watch the energy move down into the fingers. It will focus on one finger to start with, and make that finger tingle. Just so that you can become aware of the power of your own energy, it will begin to make that one finger on that one hand tingle. Allow yourself to feel the tingling start. The tingling then will spread to the next finger, and to the next, until all your fingers are tingling. Gradually this tingling, this manifestation of your energy from your center, will permeate your whole hand, until your whole hand begins to tingle. Feel the presence of your energy. And realize that this is only a fraction of the energy you possess, the energy available to you from the center of your being. Rest for a few moments, and just allow your body to tell you what it is feeling right now.

Ball of Energy

Sit facing each other and holding hands. Imagine that you are holding a huge ball of pure energy, resting between you, lightly supported by your arms and hands. Allow the energy slowly to penetrate into your fingers and hands, being absorbed easily into your body. Feel it climb up through your arm and fill your skin, bones, muscles, and blood with the pure energy of the universe. Let yourself experience this new energy, an inexhaustible supply of it. Let it make you tingle, let it fill your entire body, let it tingle your feet and toes and every part of you. Finally, allow all the energy from this huge ball you are holding to concentrate on your genitals, filling them with a tingling, relaxing, warm glow. Imagine them shining with a bright light from this energy source. Allow the huge ball slowly to melt as its energy is transmitted to your genitals. Feel the transference of this energy from the huge ball to your genitals. When all the energy resides in your genitals, slowly let your hands down and reach over and rest them on your partner's genitals, seeing whether you can feel the energy buildup there.

Activating and Sharing Energy

These are a series of exercises you can use to physically stimulate energy in your body.

Rapidly flick your fingers against the palms of your hands so that the tips touch the center of your palms. Both partners do this until it becomes tiring. When you stop, bring the fingertips of one hand slowly toward the fingertips of your other. See if you can feel something between them as they get closer, some kind of energy flow. Then, flick the fingertips rapidly again, and move them, when you stop flicking, toward your partner's hands, seeing if you can feel something happening between your fingertips and those of your partner.

Vigorously clap your hands until they get tired. Then bring your palms toward each other, and see if you can feel some kind of energy flowing between them. Then clap some more, and move your hands, palms outward, toward your partner's hands. See if you can feel something happening. Then clap some more, and move your hands toward your partner's genitals, and see whether you can sense the hands approaching, whether your genitals can feel something coming from the hands.

Don't worry if you don't feel any strong sensations of energy during these exercises. They may take practice. If you enjoy them, *continue them. If not, don't.*

Take turns vigorously tapping all over the surface of your partner's body with your fingertips. Spend at least a full minute doing this. Then stop for a moment, and, without talking, switch roles. Then hug each other and see how this feels. Share your feelings with each other about these exercises.

Music Funnel

Music is energy, actual energy vibrations of sound. Music has been used for thousands of years as a stimulus, and only recently has been rediscovered as a mood- and energy-transformation device. This is an experience in listening to music in a new way, with your genitals.

You may lie side by side with your partner and hold hands, or lie head to head, with the tops of your heads touching.

Each person raises the left knee so that it is sticking straight up while the left foot is flat on the floor. The right ankle is then brought up and rested on the bent left knee. As you can see, this creates a sort of funnel effect, leading straight to the genitals. Play some favorite music, preferably something with a strong beat. Imagine it coming right through that funnel and into your genitals, and thus energizing them and washing them in a warm bath of sound vibrations. When your genitals are feeling energized, and you have a clear image of the music being absorbed into them, allow the music energy to move on up your body and out the top of your head. If you are lying head to head, this will have an interesting effect: as the music leaves your body and enters your partner's head, your partner's music comes into your body.

Listen to My Heart's Song

Sit facing each other. Start very tenderly caressing your partner's genitals. Your partner allows arousal to happen, but then focuses that sexual energy into the heart, imagining it flowing up into the heart. At the moment the person being stroked feels that the energy has reached the heart, he or she says to you, "Listen to my heart's song."

Keeping at least one hand on the genitals, you then lean forward and place your head against your partner's chest, your ear against the heart, and listen to the heartbeat. You may also feel the connection between the sexual energy generated at the genitals and the heartbeat or "heart's song." After a moment of quiet reflection, switch roles.

The Energy Jump and Cuddle

A number of primitive tribes use jumping as a means of generating energy, whether for lovemaking, harvesting, having a festival, or going to war. Jumping wakes up the body and enlivens the spirit. This exercise allows you to share the results by tuning into each other's body responses.

Standing separately, each partner jumps as high as possible into the air and lets out a mindless yell. You may do this with eyes open or closed. When you land, be quiet for a moment, and then jump again. Do it for a total of three jumps and yells. You'll begin to feel some responses in your body. Come together in a comfortable cuddling position, making contact in as many places as possible while maintaining optimum comfort. Be aware of your partner's breathing and body temperature, and whatever else you can perceive in his or her body. Stay as motionless as possible without creating any tension in your body. If something absolutely needs to be moved or stretched, by all means move or stretch it. Stay together like this for as long as you can. If you could possibly do it for an hour, you may be surprised at some of the sensations you experience.

Body Music

For this exercise, you need some massage oil and body powder, and a towel.

While this is a form of massage, it is primarily an experience in using the body as a musical instrument. Choose music that has a definite beat to it. Your partner lies down and relaxes with eyes closed. You take some oil in one hand and warm it by rubbing both hands together.

Now take a moment to allow the music to penetrate your consciousness. Imagine that you are a musician playing this particular selection. Your instrument is the body before you. Place your hands on the body and allow the music to guide them. Rub, caress, tap, massage as the music dictates, getting into the music, sharing the rhythms with your partner through your hands. When you've covered most of the surface of one side of the body with the oil, take the towel and softly wipe over the body, also in time with the music. Then sprinkle body powder over the body, and start rubbing it in, in time with the music. When this is finished, ask your partner to turn over, apply some more oil to your hands, and start the whole process over. Oil, then towel, then powder. Rest a few minutes when you are finished. Then switch roles.

The Energy Stroke

This is a technique borrowed from some of the Eastern martial arts. The idea is that you have a natural energy flow upward in your body, and that stroking down can diminish this energy, while stroking up stimulates and replenishes it. You can try a little experiment to check this out. Have your partner stand with one arm sticking out at a slight angle from the shoulder. Your partner tries to resist as you try to force that arm down to the side. Be aware of how much strength it takes to lower the arm. Then, in flowing, smooth motions, take the palm of one of your hands and glide it down your partner's body from just under the chin to just below the navel, in a sweeping action. Do this three times. Then try the arm-lowering again. You may find that this downward stroke diminishes your partner's ability to resist the lowering of an arm. If so, your partner should lower his or her arm while you stroke upward from below the navel out under the chin three times. See if this doesn't increase the resistance back to normal.

The energy stroke exercise we will use here is simply to take two hands and place one at the base of the spine, the other just above the genitals, and smoothly stroke upward. You may do this sitting, kneeling, or standing. Do it several times, and tell each other how it feels and whether it does seem to be energizing.

The Bed Dance

This is a sharing experience using music as an energy stimulus. Lie in bed together and play some rhythmic music, the kind that inspires you to get up and dance. Lie side by side, your bodies touching. Allow the music to come in and move certain parts of your body. For example, you may start out moving the foot next to your partner's foot, as if the two feet were dancing together. Allow your arms and hands to move in the air, and your hips to start moving. Let the music guide you in this horizontal dance; get lost in it as you would get lost in the beat out on a dance floor. Play with it and have fun with it. When the song is over, just hold each other in a warm embrace, feeling the energy in each of your bodies.

The Energy Hum

This is an exercise in using a sound you create within your body. Sit facing each other and join hands after crossing your wrists. Make sure you do your hand-holding in a comfortable position. Close eyes. Begin to hum softly. (You may want to select a quiet, flowing piece of music to hum to. Some people seem to enjoy some of the albums of Tibetan bells or Tony Scott's Music for Zen Meditation *for this purpose.) Allow the hum to create a vibration throughout your body. Inhale as you please. Do not attempt to match your partner's hum; this will happen naturally.*

Visualize your body as a hollow tube or empty vessel, filled only with the vibrations of your hum. Allow the hum to become automatic, so that you are not forcing it but it just emerges from your body. Allow your body to move if it wants to, as long as the movements are slow and smooth. If possible, continue the humming for about half an hour. Then, just hold each other and tune into each other's energy level.

Sending Sexual Energy Up

Sit back to back with your partner. Sit quietly for a few moments, feeling the pressure of your partner's back against yours. Become aware of your partner's breathing and the movement this creates in his or her body.

Place your hands on your own genitals and begin caressing and stroking yourself to arousal. Take your time. When you feel you are sexually aroused, just rest your hands there and feel the energy. Try to imagine sending this energy up from your genitals, along your spine and out through the top of your head. If you can feel it, fine. If not, just imagine it happening. After focusing on this for a moment or two, get a sense of your partner's presence and the fact that she or he is also attempting to send this sexual energy up through the body and out the top of the head. Just experience whatever this awareness feels like together.

Bathtub Meditation

This is done in a bathtub filled with water. Your partner leans back against the tub, while you recline against him or her, with your head slowly sliding down so your ears slip just below the water. Remain in this position for several minutes. It's a unique feeling. A stronger connection can be made if your partner places his or her hands on your forehead, as in the drawing.

When several minutes have passed, slowly come up and, without speaking, switch roles.

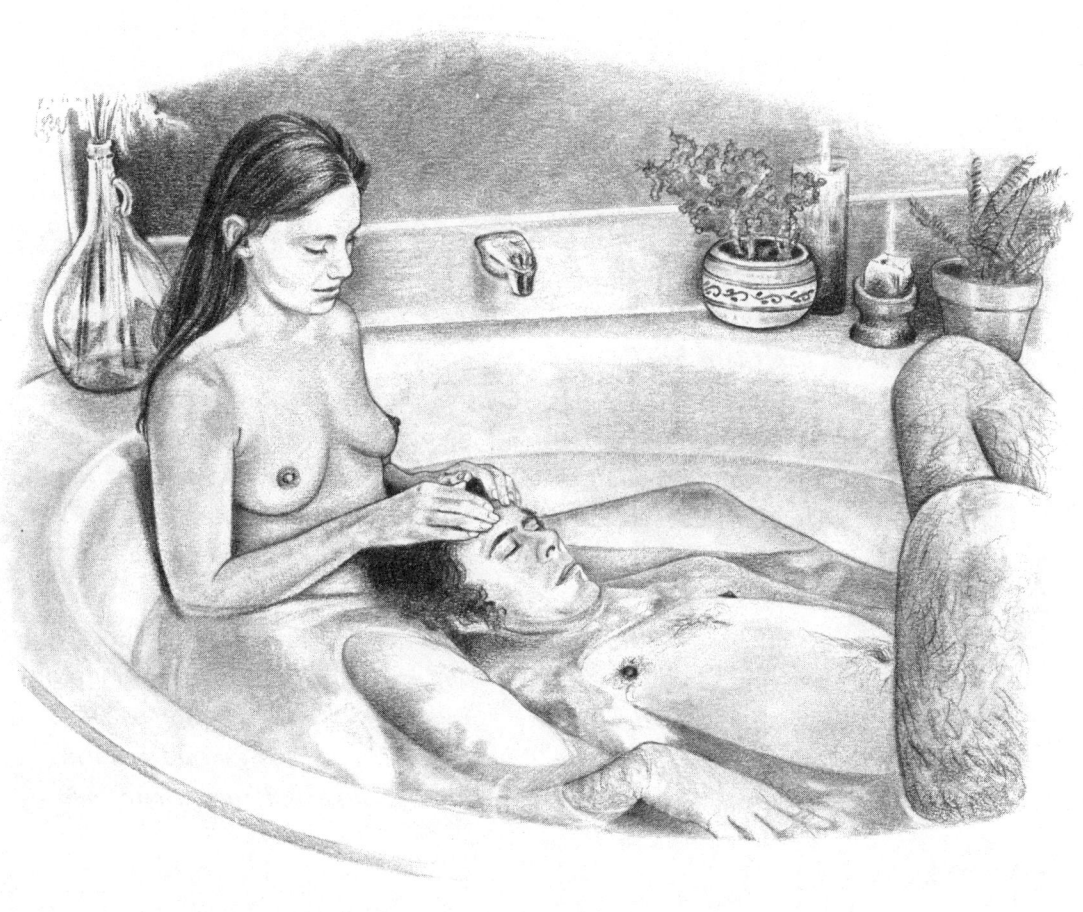

Shaking

This starts out as an individual exercise, and it might be less inhibiting if you stand at some distance from each other, facing in opposite directions. Close your eyes, though you may want to open them briefly once in a while to see what is happening. Start shaking your whole body. You might imagine it as a giant bowl of Jell-O trembling all over. Shake vigorously and continuously. Don't forget your hands, your feet, your face and head. Shake them all. Allow your body to become liquid, to vibrate with the shaking. Really get into it.

After you have been shaking for about ten minutes, just stand quietly for a moment or two and notice whatever is happening in your body. Then, open your eyes and slowly walk toward your partner. If your partner's shaking is still going on, just quietly watch. If it seems to be going on much longer, you may gently reach out and rest your hand on your partner's forehead to let her or him know it is time to stop. When your partner has stopped shaking, silently embrace, feel each other's body, and notice any effects from the shaking. Very slowly, sink to the floor together and curl up in a cuddling bundle of shared energy and love.

5

TRANSCENDENTAL AROUSAL

This is not a chapter about foreplay, though its purpose is to help you discover new ways of sensually and sexually stimulating yourself and your partner. The dictionary says foreplay is sexual stimulation intended as a prelude to sexual intercourse. In Transcendental Sex, arousal can be defined as the stimulation intended to please both parties, without worry about whether it's eventually going to involve someone's penis residing in someone's vagina. Arousal can take place before, during, after, or *instead* of sexual intercourse. All depending on how you and your partner feel at the moment, where you want it to go, what feels good. The more rigid your sexual agenda—the attitude that first there is foreplay, then intercourse, then afterplay—the less room there will be in your love life for that special quality known as spontaneity. This rigid attitude toward foreplay also creates a negative emotional impact, since it suggests that one must stop having fun and get down to serious business when it's time for intercourse. As sensitive interaction replaces goal orientation, all sexual activity becomes play, with an awareness that trying to run one's love life on a strict timetable makes it as exciting as a late-night bus ride.

Part of the problem has been our rather limited perception of the process of sexual arousal. Many people have little or no knowledge of their sexual anatomy or of what happens during arousal. Women's breasts slowly increase in size during arousal; the aureolas—the pigmented areas around the nipples—swell; and the nipples harden. The clitoris increases in size. The inner vaginal lips get thicker. The outer lips, in a childless woman, thin out and flatten outward. In a woman who has given birth, the outer lips become fuller, increasing in size. The vagina secretes a lubricating material from the vaginal walls, and this substance coats the entire vagina. As excitement increases, the inner two-thirds of the vaginal walls lengthen and expand. The cervix pulls up away from the vaginal outlet, and the uterus is also pulled up.

For the man, arousal causes the penis to become filled with blood, thickening and lengthening it into erection. The head of the penis becomes more sensitive. There is some tensing and thickening of the scrotum, and the entire sac usually moves upward toward the base of the penis. A two- or three-drop secretion may escape involuntarily from the opening in the head of the penis. These secretions are similar to those that lubricate the vagina during arousal, and are not a sign of lack of control on the part of the man.

Several emotional factors have locked us into a very narrow awareness of our full sensual potential. Strangely enough, most people take arousal as a signal to go on to the next step, rather than as direct physiological evidence that the body is enjoying what is happening at that moment. Tied into this is the belief that arousal is an opportunity that is difficult to recapture if it is allowed to pass. The more insecure someone is, the more this belief prevails. Guilt or fear about sex often leads people to rush through the whole thing as if to get it over with as quickly as possible. These feelings are usually at an unconscious level, so that the man or woman isn't really aware that such sexual patterning is a result of deep-rooted psychological barriers. And if the fears are connected with the anticipation of failure, anxiety develops, which always overshadows and may even obliterate pleasure. Not to mention the fact that expecting failure almost guarantees it as a self-fulfilling prophecy. The Transcendental Sex view, in fact, is that there is no such thing as sexual failure. Say you and your partner have a very enjoyable period of arousal and proceed to sexual intercourse, and then for some reason the man loses his erection. You really have to be goal oriented to discount that loving arousal and call the entire episode a failure. What may have happened is simply that the man's body was telling him that it did not need sexual release, that the touching and stroking were enough at that particular moment. In Transcendental Sex, arousal is, more than anything, listening to the messages your body is sending you.

Arousal is a manifestation of the ebb and flow of sexual energy, and something to be enjoyed for itself. The person who always immediately moves on to intercourse when arousal occurs, or who goes through the motions of arousal in order to get on to intercourse, or who starts shutting off the arousal because it *may* lead to undesired intercourse, is someone who is missing out on a wide range of possibilities. Sex therapists today often recommend that couples spend an evening stroking and touching and arousing each other, agreeing at the beginning of the evening that they will not have intercourse or any other form of sexual release. This tunes the couple in to the sensual aspects of their interaction, which are very often neglected and stagnant. It also removes much of that emotional smoke screen that blurs pleasure by focusing on the anticipated "main event."

In my workshops on sexuality, people have said that, for them, the best parts of sex are the initial touching and "turning on," and the moment of release or orgasm. I ask them to look at that reality. If true, then the beginning has to provide more pleasure than the end, if only because it lasts longer. Sex therapists, great lovers, and revered Eastern masters all say the same thing: The more you enjoy the beginning of sexual activity, the more satisfying you will find the total experience. Bhagwan Shree Rajneesh, the great Indian spiritual teacher, says, "There are two parts in the sexual act: the beginning and the end. Remain with the beginning. The beginning part is more relaxed, warm. But do not be in a hurry to move to the end. *Forget the end completely.* Keep attention on the fire in the beginning." And what will happen if you follow this advice is quite remarkable. It will no longer even matter if you get to the end; the beginning itself will become a total release of love and sexual energy.

What's Your Hurry?

The next time you're involved in sexual arousal and find yourself rushing toward orgasm or intercourse, just stop and ask yourself, "Why am I hurrying?" There are any number of reasons why we rush toward orgasm. We may be avoiding the pleasure and excitement of arousal, feeling that it cannot be justified unless it leads to something. We may feel rushed for time, feeling that if we don't get it all in right away, we won't be satisfied. The truth is, of course, that we can allow ourselves to be satisfied by the arousal itself. In addition to the pleasure this provides, it frees us sexually and takes the burden off subsequent sexual acts. It takes sex out of the category of duty, in which you feel that you are entitled to an orgasm or that you owe your partner one.

When I conduct workshops or classes for singles, I suggest that they remove much of the confusion and anxiety in the initial stages of interaction by making a clear statement that, at this time, there will be no sexual release. Usually, if done on a first date, even with two people obviously sexually attracted to each other, it allows them to explore each other with more warmth and less tension, so that when sex happens it is a much richer, more sensitive experience. A participant in one such workshop related the following story.

He'd had a first date with someone he'd known slightly before, he said. He and his companion had always been attracted to each other, so it seemed to him logical to assume that they would engage in sexual activity. They ended up back at his apartment and cuddled up together and began touching and kissing and turning each other on. He remembered having a distinct dichotomy of feelings. On the one hand, he wanted to continue the touching and kissing. On the other, he was concerned about possibly frustrating her, or having her think that something about her was preventing him from moving on to sex. He didn't know how to communicate this to her, and they probably would have gone on to sexual intercourse if she hadn't made a very clear statement. She said, "I'm really enjoying being with you, but I don't want to get into sex tonight. I'd like to have sex with you, but right now I'm enjoying getting to know you, and I'm in no hurry." He told her he felt exactly the same way, and they ended up sleeping together, curled up in each other's arms. Now, they could have had sex that night, and it probably would have been enjoyable, but I think they would have missed a great deal by rushing on. As it turned out, they spent every night that week together, and, by the third night, were sensitive enough and familiar enough with each other's body to have a spectacular lovemaking session.

Those precious moments of getting to know someone's body and responses before sexual intercourse are over all too quickly as it is. Why in the world rush the process?

The Purpose

There is a difference between having a purpose and having a goal. In Transcendental Sex, arousal is designed to help you overcome your dependence on and attachment to a goal, so that you can enjoy the current event rather than comparing it to a past event or worrying about what's coming next (or who's coming next). But arousal does have a clear purpose. And that is to provide pleasure for yourself and your partner in the present, to sensitize your mind and body so that whatever happens is experienced in a fully awake, alert, and perceptive state of consciousness, allowing you to learn what feels good for you and for your partner as you discover each other's sensual potential. The exercises for this chapter will no doubt give you some new physical sensations, and this can't help but enhance your sexual relating skills.

Another part of the purpose is to understand that arousal can come and go without frustration, that sex is a total body experience rather than something that only occurs in the genitals, and that the more you pay attention, the more you will feel.

In a massage workshop I was leading, a rather shy man came up to me and, obviously suffering from anxiety, said, "I purposely picked one of the most attractive women in the group to be my partner, but when she started stroking my nude body I got an erection. I tried to make it go away by thinking of all sorts of things, but it wouldn't go away, and I hardly felt the massage, and couldn't enjoy it at all since I was so embarrassed." This man had missed a wonderful sensual experience, just because his genitals didn't want to be ignored and were being awakened along with other parts of his body. In my massage workshops, we avoid genital contact, not because there's anything wrong with it, but because it's usually the other parts of our body that are suffering from the most touch deprivation. But, as I told this worried man, when the body is feeling good, it feels good all over. If he had checked himself out when his partner was stroking him, he would have found that it wasn't just his penis that was enjoying the sensations. And if he had not started worrying about it and feeling guilty, his erection would have quickly subsided. With his permission, I mentioned his fears to the group and asked for feedback from the women as to whether they would have felt threatened by his erection. There were seven women in that group, several of whom had never done a nude massage workshop before, and every one of them said that she would have been somewhat flattered by his erection, and perfectly comfortable in the knowledge that since this was a nonsexual experience his erection was not going to lead to sex. In fact, some of the women said they felt much freer touching their male partners in the nonsexual context of the workshop, and thus were able to get into the touching without worrying about whether it would frustrate the man or lead to a seduction attempt. Interestingly enough, erections are a rarity at massage workshops. If they occur, they usually disappear quickly, unless they are allowed to create anxiety. And if, as often happens, a man asks me at the beginning of the workshop what he should do if his penis gets hard, I answer, "Enjoy it, and remember that whatever goes up must come down, whether you do anything about it or not!"

The Sensual Mouth

The mouth is very much a part of sensual and sexual activity. It is multifaceted in this regard. Sharing a meal can be a peak sensual experience, and, in fact, the modern use of kissing as a sign of affection and attraction evolved out of the primitive practice of a mother chewing food and then feeding it from her mouth to her child's mouth. Kissing is usually a prelude to lovemaking. The mouth is also the vehicle for speaking gentle words of love to another person. It seems a most natural progression for the mouth to become involved in arousal and sexual activity. But many people have a major emotional block concerning what is generally described as "oral sex," usually motivated by some feeling that the genitals are dirty and disgusting. As we noted in chapter 3, this attitude has a powerful inhibiting effect on sexual fulfillment. Usually, the genitals are cleaner and more germ-free than either the mouth or the hands, so most of the negative feelings about "oral sex" are fantasy fears.

Rather than using the term "oral sex," which sounds so clinical, let us explore instead the pleasures to be derived from a "loving mouth." The more you see sex as a celebration of life and sharing of the universal life force, the more comfortable you will be about using your loving mouth to please and satisfy your partner. If you have some negative feelings about this, one of the first steps in overcoming them is to allow yourself to discuss them with your partner. A sensitive partner will respond not by saying "That's a silly attitude," but by making a verbal or nonverbal statement to the effect that "I understand you are uncomfortable with this. Take your time, and together we will tenderly explore the possibilities."

Even if you have a liberated awareness of the delights of the loving mouth, there's a strong likelihood you have been limiting yourself in terms of the many pleasurable sensations available to you. If, for example, you've only used your mouth to arouse your partner, paying primary attention to his or her state of arousal rather than how that body feels and tastes to your mouth, then you've been missing out on a lot of lovely sensations. One of the main advantages of the mouth as a means of expressing and receiving love is its extreme sensitivity to textures and tastes, and the subtle control you have over its movement. In one of my sexuality workshops, one young woman told the group: "I want to develop my vaginal muscles so that I can give my husband as many different pleasures and have as much control as when his penis is in my mouth."

The Sensitive Groove

You have a very sensitive area located between your anus and your genitals. This is known as the perineum, and many people neglect this groovelike space, perhaps because it is not highly visible, perhaps because of those same feelings of dirt and disgust that inhibit so much sensual interaction. Your perineum loves to be touched, caressed, kissed, and licked. It's especially nice to stroke it during intercourse or while using your loving mouth on your partner's genitals. In Tantric terminology, the perineum is known as your *Muladhara chakra.* The chakras are considered the major centers of energy in the body, and there are seven of them. The first, or root chakra, is your perineum or Muladhara. The others correspond to your genitals, your navel, your heart, your throat, the space between your eyebrows, and the top of your head. Any good book on yoga will give you more details on these energy centers and their function. For our purposes, it may be useful to know that in Tantra practice, it is suggested that the man and woman send energy, or imagine sending energy, into their own Muladhara, and then focus their imagination on their partner's Muladhara, thus psychically stimulating the energy center. Another way to stimulate the perineum is to make a conscious effort at tightening the anal sphincter muscles. You might try doing this from time to time during the course of sensual/sexual activity, just as a way of focusing awareness.

Arousal Exercises

If you want to get the most out of the following exercises, don't do them all at once, and don't do them as a substitute for traditional foreplay, merely replacing a new habit for an old one. Use your imagination. Do them together at different times. You may want to explore one of the exercises at some point when you only have a few minutes, not enough time for a total sexual involvement, but certainly time enough to give and receive some peak pleasures. Do some, if you wish, with an understanding that intercourse will follow, and others with a clear agreement that there will not be intercourse. Try some of the exercises following intercourse. A few can even be done during intercourse, pausing in your normal rhythms to focus on this new exploration, and then returning to regular sexual activity. The idea is to expand your horizons, and get away from some of the rigid patterns we have all allowed to restrict us.

Some of the upcoming exercises will lead you into totally new areas of physical interaction. This is intentional. You are forced to pay more attention to something new, rather than take for granted something old and familiar. In paying attention, you may find that you can come up with your own modification or variation of an exercise, one that will better fit the mood and physical desires of you and your partner, or one that will be more appropriate to the size and shape and characteristics of your respective bodies. Allow yourself this experimentation. It is part of the process of learning. And even if my specific instructions meet all your needs, feel free to play with them and vary them at some later date.

You can decide with your partner whether you want to read over all the arousal exercises before trying one or more of them, or let them come as pleasant surprises. You may even find that reading them together is arousing itself. You will probably get sexually excited during many of these exercises. That is not a specific goal, but it is a happy effect of sensual touching between a man and a woman. Enjoy the excitement. Just because we are focusing on sexuality as a meditation, don't block out the joy of arousal in the mistaken notion that this suppression makes you a more meditative, spiritual, or loving person. You have the priceless gift of being able to be sexually aroused, and what makes it a meditation is being able to let go and totally surround yourself with those pleasurable responses.

Arousal Communication

This exercise may be difficult if you don't have a foundation of trust and communication in your relationship. The idea is to tell each other some of the ways in which you like to be sexually aroused, and some of the most enjoyable arousal activities you have experienced in the past.

The next part of the exercise involves asking your partner to touch specific areas on your body, or do specific things. You can decide either to spend a few minutes in which only one partner is asking and the other responding, or to switch back and forth. The back-and-forth exchange might go like this:

Partner #1 "I would like you to touch my breasts very lightly."
Partner #2 Touches her breasts lightly.
Partner #2 "I would like you to kiss my neck."
Partner #1 Kisses his neck.

Arousal Feedback

One partner very slowly begins to caress and stroke and excite the other. The partner being aroused signals which strokes and caresses are most pleasurable and exciting by using the following words:

> WARM
> WARMER
> HOT
> HOTTER

When the partner being caressed feels that orgasm may be approaching, he or she signals the other to either stop momentarily or touch some neutral part of the body, and this is done by saying the word COOL.

The purpose here is to see how slowly you can move your hand and how potent this can be as a sensual tool, as well as to learn more about what turns your partner on sexually. You may want to talk about your feelings about this exercise, particularly the first time you explore it, before switching roles.

The Thumb-Sucking Exchange

This is an exercise to put you in touch with some early infancy memories and feelings of vulnerability and caring.

The experience may be enhanced by playing some soft soothing music.

Each partner lies in fetal position, not making contact but close to the other person. Each partner takes his or her own thumb in between the lips and starts softly sucking, imagining being once again a very young child. Get into the thumb sucking as much as possible, allowing a natural rhythm to develop.

At some point, when it feels right, exchange thumbs. Place your thumb in your partner's mouth and vice versa. Continue to suck.

After a few moments, take your hands away from your mouths and place them on each other's genitals, lightly cupping them. In another minute or two, embrace and hold on to each other, imagining that you are being held as an infant, being nourished. You may even choose to rock slightly back and forth as you hold each other.

This is a sensitizing experience, and you might check out whether it has accomplished this by stroking and caressing each other and discovering whether you have intensified your sensual perception.

Genital Oil Bath

For this exercise, you need some form of massage oil. Your partner lies down, with a towel underneath the genital area to protect carpet or sheets. Soak your hands in the oil, and then also pour a liberal amount onto your partner's genitals. Then, with smooth, caressing, gentle movements, run your hands all over the genital area, floating through the oil, covering every tiny portion of skin surface possible, including the sensitive grove between the anus and the base of the genitals. After beginning, close your eyes and let the touching become a meditation, without specific purpose; just allow whatever sensations occur to emerge. Continue this for at least ten minutes, and then switch roles, allowing a minute or two for silent reflection before beginning the process again.

Active/Passive

This is an exploration of your active and passive parts. One partner lies down, and for ten minutes or so, the other partner gives him or her as many pleasurable sensations as possible, short of orgasm. The partner lying down cannot reciprocate, and has to remain completely silent and passive, though sighs and other non-verbal sounds are okay.

When the ten minutes are up, gently switch positions, without speaking, so that the second partner is now in the passive role.

The idea is to use your imagination, to let your mind go.

Creating the Perfect Love Partner

Each partner sits or stands alone. Starting with the top of your head, slowly touch each part of your body, including the genitals, as if you were forming a perfect human being. Take your time and don't miss any patch of skin you can reach. Think to yourself, "I am creating a warm and loving person." Keep your eyes closed for most of this experience, but two or three times take a quick glance at your partner, taking in what he or she is doing as if you were taking a photograph with your eyes.

If one partner finishes the head-to-toe touching before the other, just remain silent and wait. When you have both finished, without talking, stand facing each other and place your hands on each other's head. Look into each other's eyes for a moment, and then close your eyes. Slowly begin to feel and touch every part of your partner's body, as if you were sculpting the best love partner in the universe for yourself. Don't avoid or miss any part of the body. If you have to kneel to reach the lower parts of the body, do so. When you are both finished, embrace and hold each other, realizing you have each just created exactly what you need for yourselves in the way of a perfect love partner. After a moment or two of silent reflection, open your eyes and look at each other.

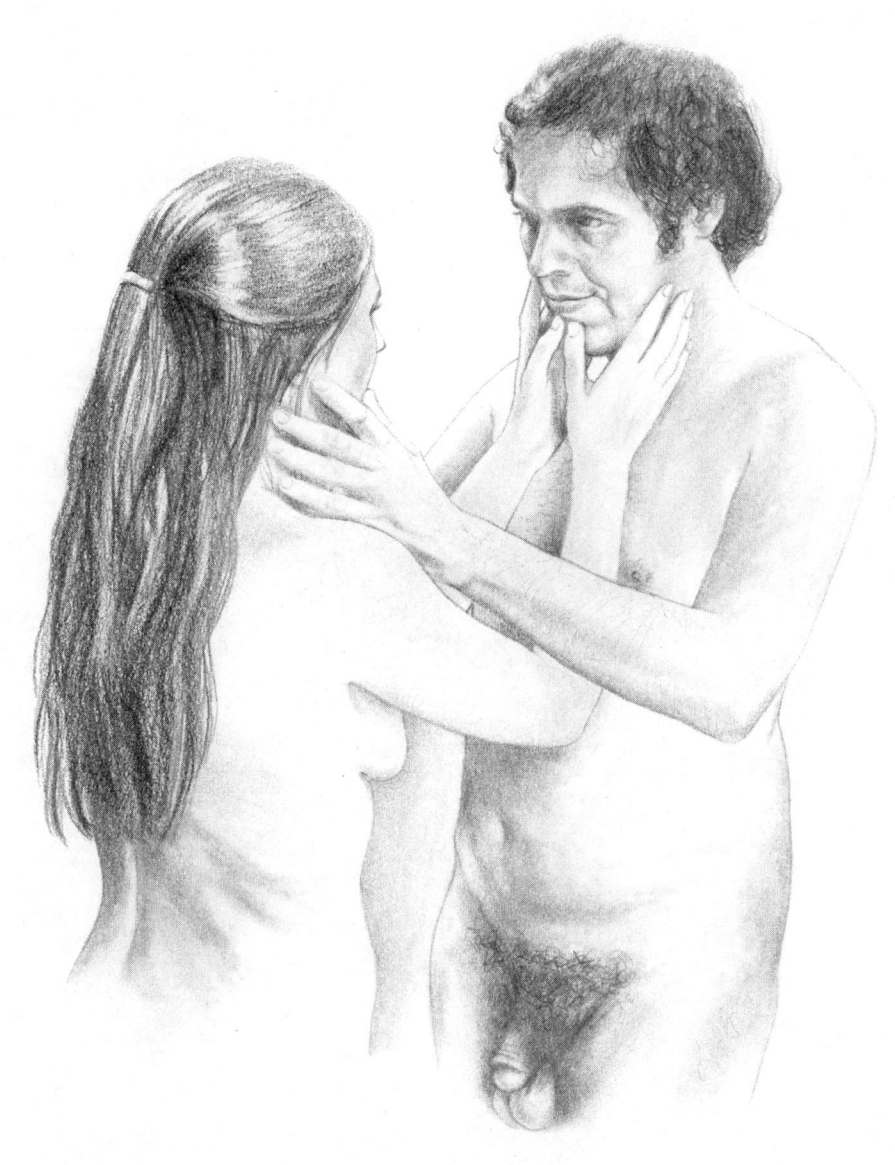

Head-to-Genital Exploration

This is an experience in getting to know your partner's genital area and giving it tender, loving attention.

Take as long as you like with this, and don't worry about getting to the other person's "turn." In fact, you may choose to have one partner play the more passive role, the other the more active, and agree to switch roles at some future time.

One partner lies on his or her back. The other lies in a comfortable position, head resting on or near the other's genitals. Look at your partner's genitals, smell them, taste them. Feel what the warmth feels like against your cheek, against your neck, at your forehead. From time to time reach out with your lips, your tongue, and even gently with your teeth, giving pleasure, taking in the sensations. From time to time just rest there, feeling your partner's energy and warmth.

You may even choose to fall asleep together in this position. Or use it in postorgasm intimacy.

The Genital Guessing Game

This is a playful little game designed to test the sensitivity of your genitals and provide you with some new and pleasing kinds of touch. It's related in some ways to the Body-Parts Contact exercise in chapter 3.

One partner lies on his or her back, eyes closed, and spreads legs so that genitals are easily accessible. The other partner then gently touches some part of his or her body to the accessible genitals. The partner lying down tunes in to the sensations and tries to guess which part of the body is making contact.

This can be fun. You can also vary it in as many ways as your imagination can think up. You can let it be more sensual and less of a game by not trying to guess the body part, but just enjoying the physical feeling.

The Feather Sweep

One partner lies down. The other very lightly, using only the fingertips, touches his or her body from head to toe, with featherlike, smooth and quick movements. Include the genitals in these feather touches, sweeping over them as you do the entire body.

The partner being touched then turns over and the feather sweep continues over the entire surface of the skin. Spend at least five minutes on each side of the body.

Then hold each other silently for a moment or two, and switch roles.

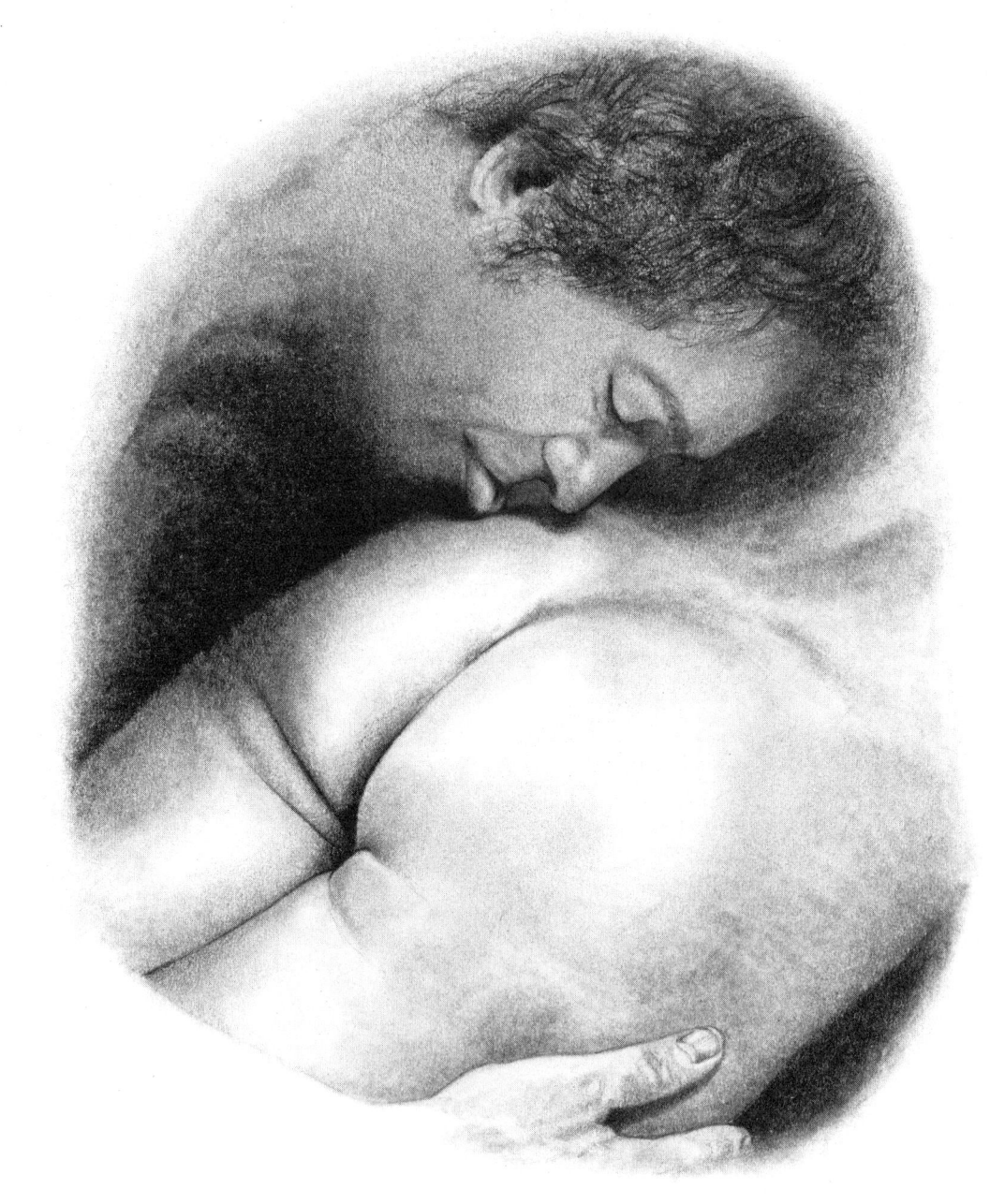

Mouth-to-Body Ritual

This is a ritualized act of love, done in a very slow rhythm. Your partner is lying on his or her back. You are sitting or kneeling. See your partner as a manifestation of all that is good and beautiful in human beings. Your partner is relaxed, with eyes closed, absorbing whatever the experience brings. Slowly look at every part of this body stretched out before your eyes, taking in all the tones and textures.

Very slowly, and very gently, begin to kiss your partner's body. Light kisses covering every inch of body surface, including the genitals.

Then, again slowly, begin to lick the surface of the body. Every once in a while, in addition to licking, very tenderly squeeze a patch of skin between your teeth, not closing the teeth, but just taking a small quantity of the body and giving an affectionate squeeze as a contrast to the slow licking action.

Next, your partner turns over and you repeat the kissing and licking.

When the entire body has been covered, hold each other in silence for a moment, and then switch roles.

This is, in effect, a worship ceremony in which each partner pays homage to the other with lips and tongue and teeth.

6
THE LOVING CONNECTION

The sexual union of a man and woman is a sacred act. Not in the sense that it is to be held in awe, but rather that it is a reaffirmation of the holy nature of life and of our appreciation for the gift of life. You do yourself a disservice when you allow this beautiful manifestation of love to be merely a physical act, without caring, without sharing. Intercourse, at its most satisfying, is a meditative form of worship. The man is worshiping all that is uniquely feminine, the woman is worshiping all that is uniquely masculine, and they are simultaneously worshiping the male and female that are in each of us.

Intercourse is an act of procreation even when it does not produce children, for each loving connection can be so potent that it becomes a form of rebirth, creating a new you, providing a fresh outlook. At its most fulfilling, it is a surrendering of ego, conditioning, roles, fears, even personality, so that the real you who lies beneath all the façades can emerge. The sex act thus gives you an opportunity to let go and be at one with nature and the universe.

Sexual union entails a powerful commitment. In order for it to reach its full potential, each partner must agree to be totally present in mind and body. This commitment is reinforced by the nature of the sex act itself, which promotes an intensified awareness of the present. This is really the core of meditation: focused awareness of the present moment.

Love is the most powerful "now" experience there is. The deeper the love, the more present each person can be. Sex is, therefore, always much more enriching when coupled with love. Sex without love is rather dehumanizing. In conducting workshops for people just out of marriages and other long-term love commitments, I have found that there is often a period of frantic sexual exploration following the end of a major relationship. These people report, almost without exception, that such sexual episodes are not fulfilling or nourishing. One woman described feeling as though she had a bad taste in her mouth that had spread all over her body. The reason for this dissatisfaction is simple. These people, feeling lonely, are trying to find love with their genitals. It just won't work. It may, however, be a healthy cleansing experience, one that can help the healing process and, if nothing else, sharply demonstrate that sex without love is hardly elevating.

Everyone seems to agree that sex as an expression of loving feelings is much more desirable than sex without love. To go a step further, there are certain ways of loving that are healthier and happier. For example, the fewer conditions placed on love, the freer we are to be loving. When demands and expectations are placed on the other person, his or her freedom to share fully is limited. Asking someone, "If I love you now, will you promise to love me tomorrow?" is making a demand of that love, rather than just letting it happen.

The fewer conditions, the more love. All demands and conditions are future oriented and goal directed, and they take us away from the moment. Love is a current event. You can only make love in the now, in the moment. Anything else becomes less than love. Our fears get in the way of love. If during a loving moment of passion you are worrying about whether your partner will eventually leave you, at that moment you are not loving, you are worrying. The human consciousness only has room for one primary focal point at a time, and a negative thought or feeling can often wipe out a positive one merely because we give it that power. As soon as the holding on to someone becomes more important than the love, the love begins to die. Fear and love are incompatible, especially in the bedroom. Now, you're never going to be completely free of fear, completely unconditional in your love. This is a direction in which to head, not a final goal. Awareness that you may have been making some demands will in itself move you forward, past some of those demands. One question to ask in preparation for tender sharing is, "Am I demanding something, or am I just willing to love and be loved, however that may happen?" *Let* is an important word here. Let love. Let the other person be. Let yourself feel. Let demands and conditions fly out the window. Let go. Interestingly enough, in conducting hundreds of workshops on love and relationships, I have found that those men and women who have moved toward eliminating demands, conditions, and expectations from their relationships have longer lasting and more intense love experiences.

One way to appreciate the depth of the commitment and the potency of the sharing is to see the sex act as an exchange of your basic life forces. This may not be as esoteric as it sounds. Even today, we are still discovering new things about the biology and function of sex. Some highly respected scientists have theorized that intercourse may actually modify the body chemistry. In his pioneering book, *Tantra, The Yoga of Sex,* Omar Garrison wrote:

> There is the curious phenomenon called telegony—the adaptation of the female organism to that of the male.

Some years ago, Dr. Jules Goldschmidt of France put forward the theory that male generative cells not only fertilize the ovum of the female, but modify her blood chemistry.

He said the millions of spermatazoa not needed for fecundation are not lost in dissolution. Instead, activated as they are by flagella, they easily penetrate the mucous membrane of the uterus and, passing through the lymphatic and blood capillaries, enter the blood stream. . . . Evidently the Biblical assertion that the twain shall become one flesh has, like most scriptural statements, deeper meaning than has been realized.

The genetic theory of telegony asserts that a woman may have sex with one man, then subsequently have sex and produce a baby with another man, and that baby may have some of the characteristics of the first man with whom she had intercourse. This may seem quite fantastic to you, but again, we know so very little about the biology of sex. This sort of theory may account for the fact that so many couples in long-term relationships begin to take on each other's physical appearance.

In any event, during intercourse there is a great deal of physical contact, and many physiological reactions take place. To assume that this won't deeply affect each partner may well be as narrow-minded as assuming that a village on the edge of a volcano won't be affected when it erupts. And covering up the intensity of the experience won't make it go away; denying the intimacy by trying to keep it light and casual won't take away from the fact that intercourse is an inherently intimate experience.

The melting together of two persons into one may therefore be more than a spiritual or emotional concept. There is also the psychophysiological principle that for each physical change in the body, there is a corresponding mental-emotional change, either conscious or unconscious, and for every mental-emotional change, there is a corresponding and appropriate physiological response. The mind and body are irrevocably intertwined. Every sexual act therefore affects your mental-emotional state, and your mental-emotional state affects every sexual act—still another good reason to be lovingly aware, relaxed, and emotionally calm before sharing sexual energy with another person.

You may find it rather farfetched to look at the sex act as a way of absorbing a part of another person into your system and having the other absorb a part of you. Great religions have, however, been teaching this as a basic truth for thousands of years. And perhaps the reason we've gotten away from it as an accepted belief is that we have rebelled against the dehumanizing strictures offered in conjunction with it by the religions. It is one thing to see sexual union as a sacred act, a blending of energies, a coming together of the universal life force. It is quite another to say that this means sex should be used only for producing offspring, and that you must have only one sexual partner for the entire span of your life.

Actually, the most useful role of this concept, whether you accept it fully or reserve judgment, is that it may help you become more selective. Selective in choosing a sexual partner, and selective in the ways in which you approach that partner, in the degree of sensitivity and caring you allow to become a part of your sexual functioning. So whether you believe it or not, accepting the possibility will make you more careful, and more care-full.

Position Isn't Everything

It's been said that position isn't everything in life. Well, it's certainly true that position isn't everything in love, but it would be difficult to believe this if you allowed yourself to be influenced by many of the so-called sex manuals on the market. These books and their proponents seem to confuse lovemaking with sexual acrobatics, their hypothesis being that the more sexual technique you learn, the more fulfilling your sex life will be. In Transcendental Sex, technique is secondary to attitude. With a healthy and creative attitude, technique will take care of itself. Two loving people with relaxation in their bodies and adventure in their hearts will discover all the sexual positions that are exactly right for them. Therefore, this is not a book about sexual technique, though there are a few sexual positions discussed and illustrated in this chapter. There's a good chance you have used some of these basic positions; indeed, they can be found illustrated on temple walls thousands of years old in the East. The reason I've included them in the book is that they are basically positions of comfort and relaxation, with a balance of weight distributed between the man and woman, thus allowing connections of longer duration. They also enhance the energy exchange discussed in chapter 4, allowing an uninhibited flow between the man and woman.

Again, what separates Transcendental Sex from ordinary sex is being aware of what is happening, allowing yourself to feel both physically and emotionally, and trusting your partner enough to let go completely. The healthiest way to experience sexual union intensely is to be able to let yourself go with your partner as freely and completely as you would be able to if you were alone. The less you allow yourself to be inhibited and self-conscious with another person, the more powerful your sexual relating will be. The best sex comes with freedom from conflict, freedom from any doubts that you want to be *here,* doing *this,* with *this particular person.* You owe it to yourself and your partner to minimize such conflict as much as possible. This is accomplished through the meditative and energizing exercises described in the preceding chapters, and by your willingness to be human and vulnerable.

During sexual intercourse, you are sharing love. This doesn't necessarily mean you are *in* love with your partner, but it does mean that you are allowing this person to stimulate whatever love feelings are within you. The more you release these feelings, the more satisfying and pleasurable your interaction. Of course, if you allow yourself to be with someone you really don't like or respect very much, or someone you are "settling for" rather than freely choosing, then this love exchange won't happen, and you will probably find the sexual performance disappointing and frustrating. If you love yourself in nourishing and healthy ways, you will take care of yourself in how you choose someone with whom to share this loving connection.

The Basic Tantra Position

This is known as the maithuna position, and it is the position most commonly used in the basic Tantra ritual. This involves the man and woman lying with the penis inserted in the vagina but completely motionless for thirty-two minutes. The couple are supposed to visualize the exchange of sexual energy between them, particularly between the points of contact at the genitals. If done in a truly relaxed state, somewhere near the thirty-second minute a violent involuntary body contraction takes place. This is not necessarily an orgasm, but is satisfying in its own way, resulting in a great feeling of unity. You may choose to experiment with this, or just to use this as a very relaxing and comfortable position for sexual union.

The man lies on his left side facing the woman's right side (the Tantra instructions call for this position because it creates a certain energy flow, but you may wish to explore reversing sides). The woman is lying on her back and raises both legs by bending her knees and lifting the knees toward her chest with her hands and arms. The man then moves his lower body around under her legs, while his upper body moves away from her, and he brings his penis into contact with her vagina. She then lowers her legs, and he places *his right leg between her legs. Slowly and comfortably, the sex organs are then brought into close contact. The man gently parts the labia of the woman and inserts his penis. This is one of the most comfortable positions possible, and it allows the loving connection to be maintained if the man's erection subsides.*

Lying/Loving Together

This is one of the most sensitive positions. Like the Sitting/Loving Together position described on the next page, it has the man and woman in similar postures. It is very comfortable and can be maintained for long periods of time, even if the man's erection disappears.

The man inserts his penis in the woman's vagina from the rear, as they both lie on their sides facing the same direction.

This position allows fluid, flowing movements of each partner's pelvis. The man can reach around and caress the woman's clitoris or breasts, or just affectionately touch her. She can reach back and caress whatever parts of his body she can reach.

Sitting/Loving Together

This is another position often used in Eastern meditative sexual practices because of its comfort and the balance between the man and woman. The couple sit facing each other, with the woman's legs over the man's thighs and around his sides. Her knees are bent so that she feels comfortable and free from tension. A sensual way to approach this position is to sit a few feet apart and slowly move toward each other, touching and stroking as you come within reach, and very slowly embracing, arousing, connecting.

The more developed the woman's vaginal muscles, the more pleasurable this particular position will be, as there is not a lot of physical movement possible between the two partners. The movements and thrusts are very subtle.

The Loving Woman

This is a particularly comfortable position for both partners, though some experimentation may be necessary to find the best balance points and most effective distribution of weight.

The man lies on his back; the woman sits astride him. Her knees are bent. This position gives the woman more maneuverability than any other, and perhaps deeper vaginal penetration. She can lean back on her hands, or move forward against his chest. The man can make thrusting movements upward with his pelvic muscles, but the movements are primarily the woman's responsibility in this position.

Stop and Focus

In any of the preceding illustrated positions, or in any of your own favorites, try a new pattern in your lovemaking. During intercourse, at some point before either partner has reached orgasm, both stop all movement, still maintaining the connection. Focus attention on the energy at the genitals. Each partner pays attention to the physical feelings in and around the genitals. Then, see whether you can imagine that energy flowing all over your bodies, washing over them as a warming tide of pleasure.

Very slowly, after a few motionless minutes, start caressing each other with your hands, and then slowly start pelvic movements again, moving so slowly you can imagine yourself in a slow-motion dream. You will be extremely sensitized at this point, and may even experience some body trembling from stored-up energy. Just enjoy whatever happens.

A Night Together

Many people talk about spending a night together, but few really do it, at least not actually together. You might want to explore this as a new and satisfying experience.

This is probably most easily accomplished in either the Basic Tantra Position, or the Lying/Loving Together position. The idea is to stay together in the loving connection all night long. You may move for a while, building up arousal, and then just be quiet, as in the Stop and Focus exercise. In either of these positions, you will probably be able to maintain the connection even if the man's penis becomes soft. A little movement and it will become hard again. Perhaps the most fulfilling way to experience this is to move in sexual rhythm together, and then relax and maybe doze off for a while. When one partner wakes up, start caressing the other, gently waking him or her, and start the pelvic movements again. If orgasm happens, let it, but don't aim for it. If you do have an orgasm, you may choose to disconnect sometime during the night, or you can just stay together. Don't set a rigid goal by saying you have to stay together all night long. Enter into this with the attitude that you'll stay with it as long as you enjoy it.

Sensual Accessories

In all sexual positions, there are opportunities for sensual activity as an addition to the coital union. Freely explore these possibilities for yourselves.

You can stroke and play with each other in a great variety of ways. And don't forget that very sensitive perineum, or Muladhara chakra, located between the anus and genitals. You can kiss and lick each other during intercourse to enhance the pleasure.

A real sensual treat for both partners is for one to suck on the fingers or toes of the other.

7
LETTING GO AND AFTERGLOW

Orgasm and the period immediately following it offer unique opportunities that are too often wasted. It is a time of surrender. Surrender of your negative programming, your fears, the mask you wear to protect yourself from being hurt. Surrender to your love partner and to the deepest part of your own self, a self that, underneath all the layers of inhibition, is free and loving, responsive and vulnerable. This chapter is designed to focus your attention on the moment of orgasm, and on the moments that follow it.

Sex researchers, including the pioneering team of Masters and Johnson, have divided the orgasm process into four major sections:

1. *Excitation*—the arousal phase that was discussed in chapter 5; again, it can be enjoyed for itself, not necessarily having to lead to orgasm.
2. *Plateau* or *energy charge*—sometimes called "the point of no return," it means increased sexual stimulation to the point where it would be nearly impossible not to continue on to orgasm. It also involves more of your total body, as compared to initial arousal, which is usually more of a mental/emotional experience. Lubricating secretions and muscular contractions may start in this phase. It is also thought that this stage produces an energy charge, perhaps due to the friction involved, especially if the plateau takes place during intercourse, oral sex, or masturbation.
3. *Release* or *energy discharge*—the letting go, the actual orgasm, which is a total body experience for both sexes. During orgasm, the narrowed outer third of the vagina and the inner vaginal lips contract with a definite rhythm, which is similar to the rhythm with which the penis contracts during ejaculation.
4. *Resolution* or *afterglow*—the postorgasmic period, a recovery time during which further sexual stimulation is either not possible or not desirable. The arousal begins to subside, the involuntary movements slow down and end, and the body becomes very relaxed.

The meditative approach of Transcendental Sex will enhance all four stages. Of course, in actual sexual activity, it might be hard to distinguish among them, as they flow together.

Not Letting Go

There are a number of reasons people find it difficult to let go completely during orgasm. One of the basic fears is that you will somehow "lose control" of your mind and body, and perhaps even have that control taken over by your partner. People who are very intellectually oriented, used to staying in their heads, will particularly find it difficult to shut off the rational/logical process, and may allow their thinking to suppress sexual energy as orgasm seems about to occur. Psychologists also note that fear of falling can be a factor in creating tension as orgasm approaches, as can fear of death. There seem to be, in our unconscious minds, some connections between orgasm, falling, and death. Any intense letting go is, of course, the death of old rigidity, and this could trigger the subconscious fear that if you let go of everything—your mind, your body, your emotions—you'll have nothing left to hold on to, and thus nothing to keep you alive. The less secure the self-image, the more likely this fear.

Holding on physically can actually create pain. If you ever experience lower back pain following sexual activity, for instance, you may not have been allowing your back muscles to let go and relax, as is their natural inclination immediately preceding and during orgasm. If you've built up a good sexual energy charge, parts of the body may tremble. This frightens many people and causes them to cut off the flowing feelings. Both men and women automatically breathe deeply starting just prior to orgasm. If this is audible, some people consciously stop it out of embarrassment.

Another factor that may prevent letting go at the moment of orgasm is being too heavily focused on achieving orgasm. Rigidly putting all your energy toward that one bodily response will usually prevent you from just relaxing and enjoying it. And of course, if you are afraid you will not have an orgasm, or if you worry about having it too soon or too late, you will stifle and diminish the letting-go process. Repressing natural orgasmic vocal accompaniments like groans, moans, and other sounds for fear they will brand you as wildly abandoned or out of control is another way to cut the flow. Persisting in some sexual activity that puts you in an uncomfortable physical posture; continuing past the point of exhaustion; making love when you really aren't in a loving mood—all of these are also ways in which you deny yourself the full potential of unrestricted sexual release.

What letting go may really be about is a feeling you have within yourself that you are capable of feeling intense satisfaction, that you won't go crazy just because you temporarily suspend rational thought—and that you deserve a peak pleasure experience every time you want one!

Momentum

During the initial excitation phase you begin gradually to build sexual energy. The energy buildup begins to intensify during the plateau phase, and explodes in a total body release during the letting-go phase, in which energy is discharged. This energy buildup and discharge can create a momentum that leads to an ecstatic feeling of connection with your partner and with the universe, a feeling that all is right with the world, that nothing more is necessary for complete happiness, that you are exactly where you are supposed to be. This feeling is very similar to what is described by people who have undergone intensive meditative training when they emerge from deep meditative states lasting anywhere from three to sixteen hours. The momentum created by energy buildup and discharge can, if you don't turn it off, carry you into an altered state of consciousness as powerful and more fulfilling than any stimulated by drugs, especially since you hold the knowledge that you are still in charge of what is happening. And all you have to do is let it happen. I'm reminded of those silly cartoon chase scenes in which one creature is chasing another toward a cliff or roof edge. The character being chased runs over the edge and out into space and actually makes progress until he realizes there is nothing underneath his feet; then he falls with a resounding crash. This is a meditative message, for we get the distinct impression that he would have made it if only he hadn't looked down. Afterglow is like that. You'll make it if you don't look down, if you don't let your head get in the way.

The natural momentum carries you from orgasmic release directly into afterglow. You can interrupt this process in much the same way as you can orgasm itself, though the afterglow period is probably cut off more often than any other part of sensual and sexual activity. Whether you do it by lighting up a cigarette, making a sandwich, starting a conversation, getting up to wash, comparing this sexual experience with previous ones, worrying or wondering about your performance, or just thinking about anything at all, the interruption of afterglow is a sad loss of nourishment and an unnecessary event. Many sex therapists neglect the potential of this period in sexual interaction by simply referring to it as "resolution," a time in which to relax and build up more sexual energy for further sexual release. It *can* be a time of the most profound union, a total linking of minds and bodies and emotions that creates a spiritual bond between you and your partner.

If you continue to let your mind go, it will take you into exciting, uncharted, but completely safe states of consciousness. When I was involved in biofeedback research at the Biofeedback Institute, I found that the postorgasmic phase usually produced powerful Alpha brain waves. As I mentioned earlier these are the brain waves that correspond to meditation and are indicative of a calm and thought-free mind. Theta brain waves, an even slower frequency, were also produced. These are the brain waves you naturally produce just before falling asleep and just after awakening. Theta waves are usually associated with creativity and vivid visualization. Many people report seeing colors and all sorts of visual images following orgasm. Subjective descriptions of afterglow also include sensations of floating, losing track of time, tingling over the entire skin surface, and tremendously increased energy levels. Afterglow is, if nothing else, a potent time for regeneration. The discharge of all that built-up sexual energy has washed through your system, cleaning it, purging it of a lot of negative physical and emotional material. By giving yourself this time simply to be, without conscious thought or action, you take advantage of what may be the greatest reward of a fulfilling sexual experience.

Letting-Go and Afterglow Techniques

The upcoming exercises are a few suggestions designed to enhance awareness during orgasm and the period immediately following. The major emphasis remains on just allowing it to happen; should the techniques distract you from that, discard them. Sometimes, however, we have to use contrived methods in order to peel off layers of emotional and physical constriction. These few uncomplicated approaches should begin to do that for you. Sexual interaction is like a dance. At the beginning, you have to pay close attention to each step. Then it becomes automatic, building up to a crescendo of synchronous motion, so that you may as well be floating in space for all the effort it requires.

Letting Go Alone

As we saw in chapter 6, the healthiest way to experience sexual union intensely is to be able to let yourself go with your partner as deeply, and as freely, as if you were alone, not letting another person's presence inhibit you in any way. To check out the differences in letting go alone and letting go when you're with a partner, it is useful to explore how intensely you can let go when alone.

The idea is to find yourself a space that will give you complete privacy. There are two ways to do this exploration. One is to allow your body to move as if it were engaged in sexual union. Move, jump, scream, do whatever seems to promote total letting go for you. Forget what your partner might think, forget what society might think, forget what your parents might think. Bring your complete energy and sexual nature to this experience.

The other way to explore letting go alone is to masturbate yourself to sexual release, and allow the release to trigger this physical and emotional abandonment. Moan and yell and thrash your body around, the way it would go naturally if only you could let go that much. Let go of all control! Lose your mind! Your body will take care of you for a while.

Deep Preorgasmic Breathing

One of the ways in which people cut off sexual energy is to stifle or hold in the breath while approaching orgasm. As the body moves in sexual union, it requires more oxygen, and yet this is precisely when many people cut down on their breathing. The best breathing for sexual activity, or for any activity requiring energy, is breathing from the diaphragm. Practice this on your own. Lie on your back, place your hands on your stomach, and feel your stomach expand to fill your hands as you inhale. Your chest is also expanding as your lungs fill with energy-giving oxygen. This is a two-way street. You cannot breathe in fully without breathing out fully, not if you want the full benefits. Tension can inhibit the exhalation. So practice allowing all the air out by releasing your chest and abdominal muscles.

During sexual union, every once in a while take just a second or two to make sure you are not holding back your breathing. It's merely a question of briefly saying to your body, "Breathe in fully, let go completely." The rest is automatic. You don't have to make a great effort. Just focus awareness every once in a while. Very soon, it will become automatic. In the moments just preceding orgasm, as you feel the excitement build, allow yourself to *breathe in rhythm with the excitement. Not as an interruption, but as a flowing part of the excitation. You may even want to breathe in rhythm with your partner—again, not as an interruption, but allowing your two bodies to become one in movement and breath.*

One at a Time

One of the things that inhibits total release is worrying or thinking about what is happening with your partner, at the same time that you are experiencing your own arousal and movement toward release. This exercise is designed to give you practice at getting away from that concern.

Decide which person will have an orgasm first. Then just get into normal sexual activity, with the added awareness that you are both focusing on just the one partner reaching orgasm. The exciting part of this exercise is that it doesn't matter whether that person has an orgasm first or not! It is the decision that frees you from concern and conflict, not what actually happens. If necessary, when that person has had an orgasm, switch your focus to the other partner.

Letting the Pelvis Go

Some parts of our bodies contain a great deal of rigidity, often connected with emotional trauma, fears, and repression. The pelvis is a prime example of this. None of us move the pelvis as freely as it could be moved if it weren't for muscular rigidity. One way to loosen up this area is to practice moving it. Alone, or with a partner, put on some movement-inspiring music, something with a strong rhythm. Move your pelvis in a circular pattern. Forward, then to one side, then backward, then to the other side. In rhythm to the music. And pay attention to your breathing! You may have found yourself shutting off the breath during this movement. If so, focus attention on the breathing as well as the pelvic movement.

Try moving the pelvis as far forward as it will go, and then as far backward. In rhythmic, gentle, thrusting movements, allow this to continue for as long as it feels comfortable.

With your partner, stand together, bodies touching at the pelvis, and allow the music to guide you in a pelvic dance, sticking together so that when one moves backward, the other goes forward, and you move to the sides simultaneously.

During sexual union, you might explore putting on some rock music and allowing your bodies to move in rhythm, freeing the breathing and the pelvis.

Using Your Hands as Assistants

During intercourse, use your hands to explore each other, but also use them to assist in letting go. For example, you might hold your partner's hips and help his or her pelvis in its movements.

Spreading the cheeks of your partner's buttocks during sexual movement can greatly enhance pleasure.

Massage the small of your partner's back during sexual union. This will help in relaxation and prevent cutting off the natural release.

Place the palms of your hands over your partner's ears during intercourse. This will shut out much sound and create a meditative feeling.

If possible, reach down and stretch your partner's feet, or pull the toes, during sexual union. We often neglect this end of our bodies.

During intercourse, take one or more of your partner's fingers into your mouth and suck on them, sucking at the same rhythm as your pelvis is moving. This creates a strong energy connection between your sensual mouth and your sexual genitals.

The Shaking Release

In chapter 4, we discussed shaking as a way of releasing and building energy. This is an attempt to use this in actual sexual interaction. At some point prior to orgasm, allow your bodies to start shaking, as if they were big bowls of Jell-O, every part quivering together. Allow the sexual energy and the sexual movements to continue, but enhanced by the total body shaking. See where this takes you. If you find it diminishing the pleasure, then let it go and get back to normal activity. If you find it releases something new in you, and this is exciting, interesting, or pleasurable, allow it to continue. Experimenting and taking risks means being willing to try something that may not work. Shaking can enhance and prolong the orgasmic response, but it won't work for everybody. Try to enjoy the effort itself, whether or not you enhance the sexual act.

The Om Release

The chanting of the word om *("Ohhhhhmmmmmm") seems to have a relaxing effect on almost everyone. During sexual union, while approaching orgasm, begin to chant om together. Allow the sexual rhythms of your body to guide the tempo of your chanting, and continue chanting after orgasm for as long as it feels right and comfortable. You might vary this by each beginning your chant at the moment of orgasm.*

One benefit of chanting during intercourse is that it requires rather uniform breathing and can help you get your breathing in synchronization with your sexual movements.

The Afterglow Stretch

Immediately following orgasm, when both partners have experienced total release, allow your bodies to stretch out together to their full length, perhaps making a sound to accompany that stretching, sort of a loud stretching sigh. Allow yourselves to feel the differences in your bodies as a result of this stretch, but don't talk or think about it or let it interrupt the afterglow. Just do it and then relax together.

Afterglow Breathing

Postorgasmic breathing is every bit as important as preorgasmic breathing. Controlling or restricting the breathing following orgasm can eliminate the revitalizing, energizing effects of sexual union. If you are consistently tired after intercourse, the reason may lie in your breathing patterns. Men sometimes hold the breath during intercourse in order to avoid or hold back orgasm. This is self-defeating, as it then becomes difficult to let it go during orgasm and afterglow. Many men also attempt to control their breathing so that they won't appear exhausted to their partner, preferring to inhibit their pleasure rather than appear weak. Heavy breathing is natural and normal for both the man and woman following orgasm. Controlled breathing shuts off the oxygenation process just when the body needs it most.

The best way to avoid postorgasmic controlled breathing is to just let it happen. Let your body do the breathing it wants to do following release. The more you let this breathing come naturally, the more you will increase your energy and pleasure.

Just Being Together

After orgasm, get into a position that allows you to be relaxed and feel each other's body, tuning in to the relaxing effects of sexual release and feeling the energy that still remains in your bodies, the deep connection you have just experienced, and the sense of sharing something special.

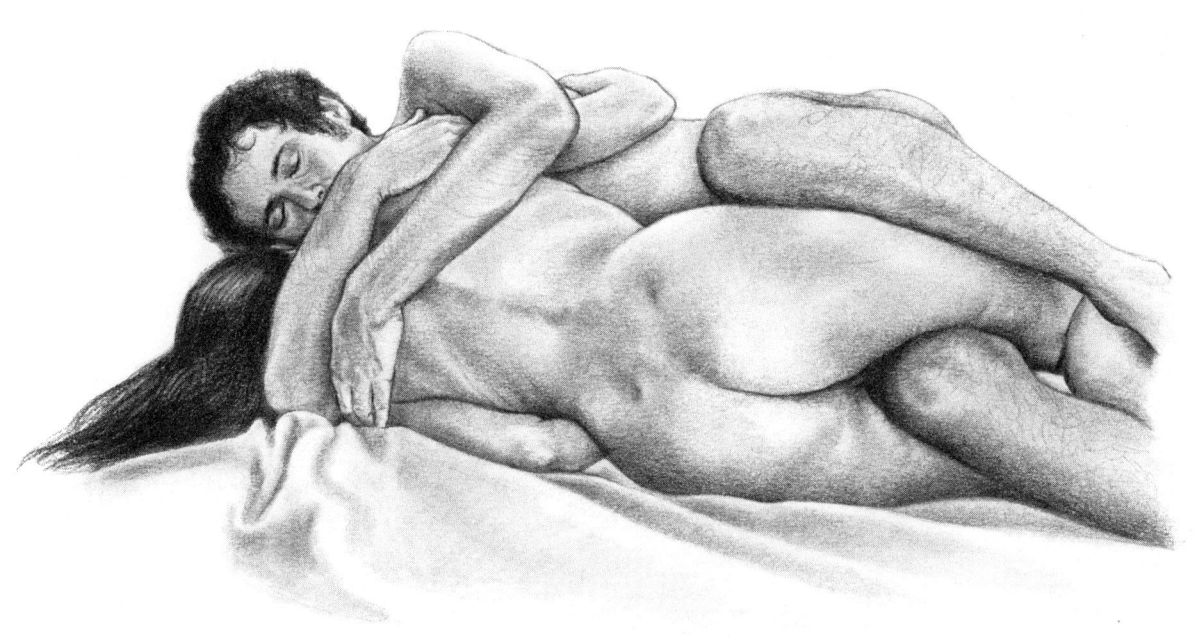

8
THE TRANSCENDENTAL SEX RITUAL

Creating a special time and place and set of actions for your sexual activity is a way of adding a new spiritual dimension to this facet of your life. In ritualized rhythm, the sex act and what precedes and follows it all come together and are elevated to the highest levels of consciousness, becoming in themselves a powerful meditation. In this book I have stressed the importance of spontaneity and freedom in sexual relating. But it can be just as liberating to vary free-flowing sexual experience with occasional ritualized encounters. Having a specific set of actions to perform creates mutual security, in that you both know exactly what is going to happen next. This structure in turn creates a special kind of freedom, in which the emotions are liberated and the mind is freed of the responsibility of worrying about or planning the mechanics of sexual interaction.

But the primary idea of a ritual is to create a mood. The particular ritual described and illustrated on these pages will create a mood of quiet excitement and intimate sharing, and a sense of the sanctity of the sex act. Love is the most precious quality of our existence, and with careful preparation, and a meditative approach, in a meaningful set of shared activities, we show our appreciation for this beautiful gift, and our respect and deep affection for our partner.

It is vitally important that we enter into sexual ritual with an open heart and complete willingness to share ourselves. This is what differentiates ritual from habit. Habit is something we do without awareness, ritual is something we do with increased awareness and appreciation. Part of the awareness of the Transcendental Sex Ritual is focused on the divine nature of man and the divine nature of woman. We honor this divinity in ourselves and each other by the worshipful attitude of the ritual. We are focused deeply inward, realizing that love is not something that comes to us from the outside, but is part of our inner consciousness. The ritual provides an environment of total comfort, one in which we feel safe enough to let those deepest parts of ourselves emerge and be revealed to our partner. The sacred quality of the union between the man and the woman is rooted in the spiritual concept that each of us is a manifestation of God, and the more loving the connection between man and woman, the closer each comes to experiencing his or her innate divinity.

Don't, however, make the mistake of actively striving for spirituality in your lovemaking. As you become more centered, sensitive, and loving, this will happen naturally. Trying to achieve it will only get in the way.

There are a number of alternative suggestions for some of the parts of the ritual. You are free to pick and choose from among them. On one occasion, you might want to begin with a drink of juice, on another wine may seem more appropriate. Also feel free to move the different parts around, perhaps moving some ahead of others, perhaps choosing to eliminate some. This is, after all, a guideline. You may find it fulfilling to go through the ritual exactly as described here, but you will probably want to modify it later to fit your own individual needs and desires.

Feelings of joyful and transcendent oneness will not happen if you do not allow yourself to feel comfortable during the ritual, or if you persist in doing it when you are tired or not in the mood. If something seems silly to you, so much so that you laugh out loud, do not stifle that laughter as if you were a schoolchild afraid of being punished. Be quiet for a while, and then decide if you are really in the proper mood for a loving ceremony. You cannot enter into this ritual out of a sense of duty or obligation or a desire to explore new thrills; nor should you embark on it casually, with a partner with whom you have no deep connection, no emotional flow. It is not to be so serious that you shouldn't enjoy every single moment of it, but neither is it to be so lighthearted that you take it for granted or just zip through it as you would a tasty pastry. You are going to focus all your attention, bring your mind and body together in full harmony, open up totally to your partner, and let go completely.

If you want to explore various components of the ritual from time to time, go ahead and borrow from it. In fact, you may not feel ready for the full experience, but this doesn't mean you can't begin enjoying some of the sensual pleasures it offers. This book has really been a preparation for this ritual. The exercises up to now have been aimed at creating an awareness of your sensual potential and your sexual energy, and the meditative quality of both.

Reading the ritual with your partner can help create the right mood, and it will also let you know what items you might need. Do not judge your performance during the ritual. It is something new for you, and thus you will not do it perfectly at the beginning. It is not meant to be a single event in your life, but the start of a new pattern in the fabric of your loving. It will get better, and you will become more sensitized, revitalized, and enriched each time you enter into this special energy exchange.

And remember, whatever you feel during the unfolding of the ritual experience is exactly what you are supposed to be feeling. It could be called a secret ceremony, not because it's kept hidden but because it can never be the same every time it is performed, even with the same two partners, and because part of the joy is in the appreciation of the mystery slowly being revealed.

Ritual Preparation

Decide which parts of the ritual you are going to share, and gather all the materials, including food, that you will need. Allow yourself as much time as possible for the ritual. Four hours would not be too long.

Choose a room in which you will be undisturbed. If possible, make sure you will not be interrupted by the phone. Candlelight is the most desirable illumination. The room temperature should be comfortable so that you can relax without having to cover your bodies.

There should be enough light in the room for you to see each other clearly, and enough air for you to breathe deeply.

You may want to light incense at the beginning. In fact, having one particular scent always associated with your sexual union is a good way to bring a sense of ritual into all your intimate interaction.

You may want to play soothing music, but choose something that will not distract.

You each might want to do an individual meditation before you come together for the ritual.

Remember: During this ritual the man is a god and the woman a goddess, and nothing is too good for either of you.

Get into the spirit of it, seeing it as a loving dance, a slow-motion ballet of sensual pleasure. Add or subtract whatever you like, but make it yours.

The Ritual Begins

Sit facing each other or leaning against each other. You may start out nude, or in some sort of robes. Fill a glass with wine or a favorite fruit juice. Alternate sipping the wine or juice and saying one of the sentences below. If the woman starts, she would sip, then say the first sentence while looking into her partner's eyes. He then sips, and says the same sentence. She sips and says the second sentence. And so on.

I AM HERE IN BODY, MIND, AND SPIRIT.

I AM HERE WITH YOU.

I AM HERE WITH LOVE.

As with all the ritual verbalizing, choose your own words if they feel more comfortable or make more sense. If you prefer, just sip the wine or juice without speaking, allowing yourself to feel your partner's presence.

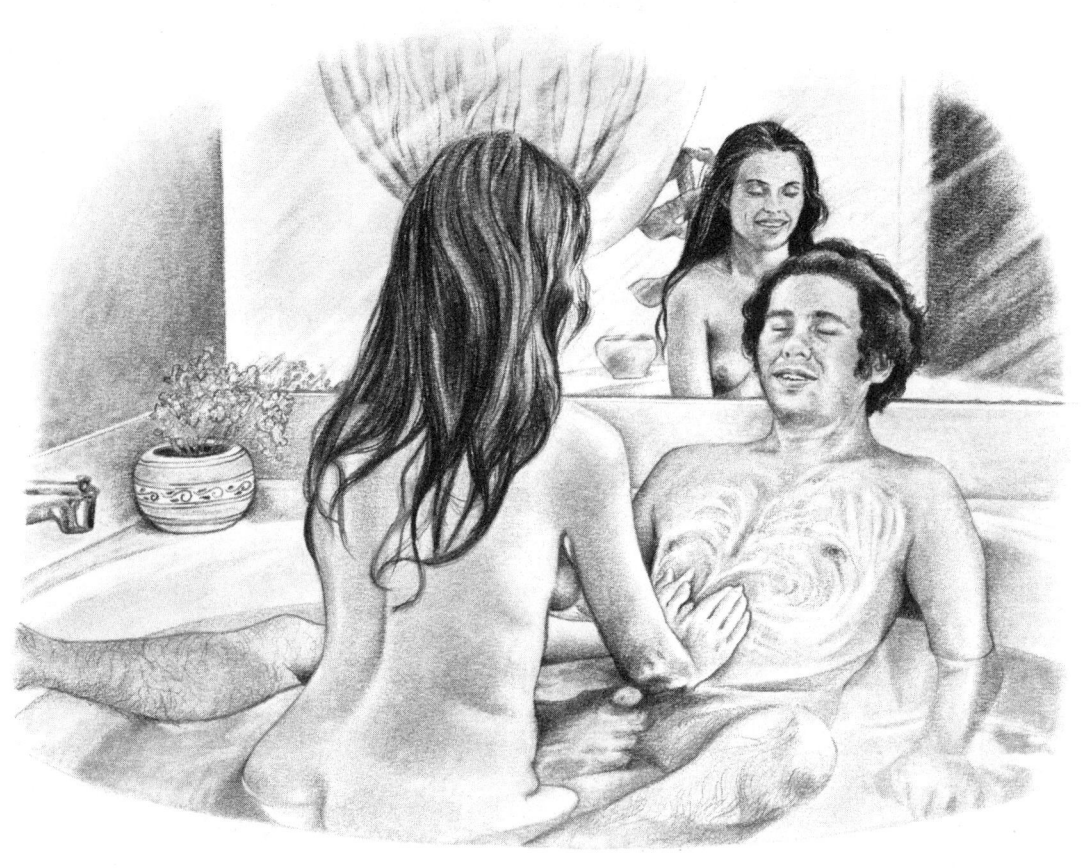

The Ritual Bath

The Transcendental Sex Ritual has a spiritually cleansing effect, and it is important that you come to it as physically clean as possible. The best way to do this is to bathe each other. Take turns soaping each other's body gently and lovingly, allowing a natural rhythm to develop between you. You can play with this part of the ritual, and intersperse the sensual touching and washing with child-like frolicking. This celebrates the child in each of us and in no way interferes with the meditative aspects or intensity of this experience. Enjoy doing whatever comes to you, and don't worry about hurrying on to the next part of the ritual. Imagine you have all the time in the world and can take as long as you want.

Anointing

This part of the ritual is performed carefully and lovingly. Anoint each other's body with some special scent you decide on together. This can be a scented massage oil, or perfume. In the Tantric rituals, musk is often used, since in its natural form it is used to sexually attract the female musk deer. Make an effort to avoid any synthetic scent. In this ritual, the important factor is to choose a scent that is pleasing to you. If possible, experiment with having incense and an oil with the same scent. This will have the effect of strongly associating the scent in your subconscious with sensual pleasure, so that eventually the mere presence of the scent can put you in the appropriate mood for love.

Gently dab the scent all over your partner's body. Do not forget the feet, the stomach, the nape of the neck, behind the knees and elbows. Be careful around the genitals and nipples, as the scent you choose may irritate these areas. (You might want to check this out before deciding on a scent. The more organic the oil or perfume you choose, the less likely it is to irritate.) Lightly anoint the root chakra, Muladhara, or perineum, located between the genitals and anus. It is traditionally believed that this very sexual area specifically responds to the stimulation of scent.

In the Tantric rituals, this root-chakra stimulation is the primary reason for using perfumes.

Throughout the anointing ceremony, use very light applications of whatever substance you are choosing. The total effect should be pleasing, not overpowering.

The Breathing Ritual

Sit facing each other. Allow your breathing to become deep and regular. This is a moment of calm reflection on how you are feeling about this ritual so far. Join hands and inhale for a count of seven together, pausing one count, then exhaling for a count of seven. This is the Seven-In/Hold-One/Seven-Out breathing exercise described in chapter 2. While you do this, concentrate on your Muladhara chakra, or perineum. Contract your anal sphincter muscles to stimulate this energy center. Once more, breathe in to a count of seven, pause, and breathe out to a count of seven. On this second breath, close your eyes and focus on sending your energy to your partner's root chakra. You may choose to repeat this a few times.

Next, hold each other in a comfortable embrace and synchronize your breathing. Tune in to your bodies and your breathing for as long as you like, or until you feel ready to move on to the next part of the ritual.

The Flower Ceremony

Choose one or more flowers you both find pleasing. Roses or hibiscus are frequently used in Eastern sexual rituals.

Sit facing each other and holding one flower between you. Look at it together for a little while. Smell it together. Rub it against your cheeks. And together, gently kiss it.

One partner lies down, and the other plucks some petals from the flower and allows them to float down onto the genitals, saying softly:

WITH THIS FLOWER, I SWEETEN THE GIFT YOU BRING ME.

When about half the petals are on the one partner's genitals, the other leans forward and smells them.

Reverse roles after a moment of quiet reflection, and repeat the ceremony with the remaining petals.

The Feeding Ritual

Ritual meals have been a part of spiritual tradition since the dawn of the human race. They enrich the spirit and show appreciation for all the good things we have in this life.

Select five or six different foods, prepare them in small, bite-sized pieces, and place these on a platter. In Tantric tradition, freshly cooked meat, fish, a cereal, and whole cardamom seeds are used. The seeds are used to sweeten the breath before the final stages of the ritual, while the other foods symbolize all the earth has to offer.

Use your imagination when selecting the foods. They can be selected on the basis of your taste preferences, but some thought ought to be given to the sensual nature of the foods you choose. It might be a good idea to choose one fruit, one vegetable, something pickled sour, bread, and something sweet, perhaps a piece of pure chocolate or a freshly baked cookie. Cherry tomatoes are particularly sensual, as they explode with juice and flavor in your mouth as you bite into them. A chunk of bread can be broken together as part of the feeding ceremony; you can visualize the golden fields of wheat that produced the bread as you share it. Do include one small fruit, perhaps a grape, seedless if possible. I suggest that at least one food item be something neither of you has ever tasted before.

Make the choice a joint effort. You can make the preritual shopping into a loving adventure by searching together in gourmet food sections. If this is difficult, you might mix two foods you've never tasted combined before. A small piece of apple with a tiny piece of sausage is one example. A chunk of pineapple with an olive is another. The idea is to have as many tastes as possible represented.

Begin the feeding ritual seated, with two pieces of each food you've chosen on a platter between you. Slowly, and with love, pick the first food. Each take a piece and feed it to your partner. Feel it in your mouth before you bite. Let the taste sensations fill all your senses. Then chew it slowly, allowing it to become a liquid before swallowing it. Continue with the next food. Have a glass of water, wine, or juice near, so that you can wash away the taste of each food in preparation for the next.

When you come to the grape, or similar substitute, lean toward each other and place it between your mouths, holding it with your lips. One partner then takes it into his or her mouth, carefully avoiding biting it. It remains there a moment and then is passed into the other partner's mouth, with the lips, teeth, and tongue doing the passing. This is a very sensual experience, so enjoy it as such. Then, with the grape resting between your two mouths, bite into it together, and eat it together.

You might want to vary the food combinations each time you experience this ritual, or you may want to keep some of the same foods, as they now have achieved a significance in connection with your lovemaking.

Symbolic Opening

Taking turns, one partner curls up into as compact a position as possible, as if he or she were a flower folding up for the night. Very slowly and gently, the other begins to unfold this human flower, so that eventually the body is spread out to receive love and nourishment.

The process is then repeated with the other partner.

See if you can't really get into the feeling that you are being opened, that you are now free from limitations and expectations and demands, and ready and willing to give and receive with your partner.

Ritual Blessing

This is an opportunity for you to bless and pay homage to your partner's total being. Your partner lies down. You say:

AND THUS I WORSHIP YOU FOR ALL THAT IS BEAUTIFUL AND HOLY IN WHAT WE ARE ABOUT TO SHARE

Now focus attention on four places on your partner's body:

The middle of the forehead, an important spiritual center.
The heart, a symbol of love.
The spot two inches below the navel, your core of energy.
The genitals, a repository of your basic life force.

First, gently rest the palm of one hand on each of these places, feeling the warmth; then slowly move on.
Then, take the same hand and place it an inch or so above each of the places, imagining all your energy concentrated in that hand and flowing into your partner.
Next, gently kiss each place.
Then, let your tongue lightly lick each place.
Finally, allow a soft current of air from your mouth to caress the four places, as you lightly blow on them.
Rest for a moment, and then switch roles.

The Ritual Connection

At this point in the Transcendental Sex Ritual, you will probably have a feeling of being joined together at many different levels. Thus, this final connection is more of a continuation of the process than a dramatic change.

The partners very slowly caress each other to arousal, or partial arousal. Choosing a position that is comfortable, perhaps one of those illustrated in chapter 6, the penis is very slowly inserted into the vagina. If it is not fully erect, do not be concerned. You may want to insert the penis only partially at this point. At the moment of insertion, say,

WE ARE ONE

Realize that your connection is born of gentleness and love. Start moving together, allowing the woman to hold the penis and slowly move it against her vaginal lips. Slowness, easiness, gentleness of spirit. Move just as much as necessary to maintain an erection, but if the erection goes away, do not force it back. What will happen is what will happen. You are sharing love; there are no rules or goals.

If orgasm happens, or if you are both satisfied without it happening, just hold on to each other, maintaining the connection, and feeling the thought,

WE ARE ONE

Repose

Whether or not you have chosen to have an orgasm, you have shared a beautiful and loving ritual together. Find a comfortable position, one in which you can remain relaxed for some time. You may want to focus on each other's breathing, perhaps synchronizing your inhalations and exhalations. Just be together, without thought, without words. These are the moments together you have been moving toward. A calm and serene sharing. An understanding of each other at a deeper level of consciousness.

In the Tantra tradition, it is believed that you are married, for that period, to whomever you open up to in a sexual ritual. In a sense, this is true. You have bound yourselves to each other for an intense awakening of your senses. Feel it as you stay together in repose.

About the Author

In 1970, after twelve years as a newsman and commentator, Jerry Gillies left NBC in New York to focus on a more personal form of communication. Since then he has developed and taught thousands of people new techniques in awareness, relaxation, meditation, and interpersonal communication. He was Founding Director of the Biofeedback Institute of New York, and he has lectured and conducted workshops for conferences of the Association for Humanistic Psychology as well as hundreds of universities, growth centers, and organizations across the country. Mr. Gillies is the author of *Friends: The Power and Potential of the Company You Keep* and *My Needs, Your Needs, Our Needs*, and his articles have appeared in a number of national magazines. Born in Philadelphia in 1940, Jerry Gillies now lives in Miami, where he teaches at Miami-Dade Community College and serves as General Coordinator for the Association for Humanistic Psychology.